GERBILS

All About Them

Alcoholism, Epilepsy, Sleep and Dreams, Life in the Universe, Unusual Partners, Rats and Mice, The Origin of Life, The Respiratory System, A Star in the Sea, A World in a Drop of Water, Cells: Building Blocks of Life, Carl Linnaeus, Frederick Sanger, Germfree Life, Living Lights, Circulatory Systems, The Digestive System, Bionics, Harold Urey, Metamorphosis: The Magic Change, Mammals of the Sea, The Nervous System, The Sense Organs, The Endocrine System, The Reproductive System, The Code of Life, Guinea Pigs: All About Them, The Long Voyage, The Muscular System, The Skeletal System, Cancer, The Skin, The Excretory System, Exploring the Brain, The Chemicals We Eat and Drink, Rabbits: All About Them, Animal Invaders, Hamsters: All About Them, Oranges, Beans, Potatoes, Apples

GERBILS
All About Them
by Dr. Alvin Silverstein and Virginia B. Silverstein
with photographs by Frederick J. Breda

J. B. Lippincott Company / Philadelphia and New York

Photographs in this book have been provided through the courtesy of the following:

Title page, pages 8 bottom right, 11, 30 right, 32, 39, 127: Tumblebrook Farm, Inc.

Pages 14, 47, 60, 82, 87 top left, 88, 89, 90, 91, 92, 93, 94, 95, 119, 121, 135, 150, 151, 152, 154: Alvin and Virginia Silverstein

Page 29: Joe Haley, Haley Farm

Pages 30 left, 140: Stephan H. Cramlet and John D. Toft II. The photo on page 140 is reprinted by permission from "Malignant Melanoma in a Black Gerbil" by S. H. Cramlet, J. D. Toft II, and N. W. Olsen. *Laboratory Animal Science*, Vol. 24, No. 3 (1974), pp. 545–547.

Pages 40 middle and bottom, 41, 42, 43, 44: Photos by Ernest P. Walker from *Mammals of the World*, 3rd ed., by Ernest P. Walker, revised by John L. Paradiso, 1975. Copyright © 1975 The Johns Hopkins University Press. Reprinted by permission.

Pages 128, 129, 131, 134, 142, 149: Delbert D. Thiessen

Page 141: Reprinted with permission from *Science News*, the weekly news magazine of science and the applications of science, copyright © 1968 by Science Service, Inc. Photo by D. G. Robinson, Jr.

All photos not otherwise credited were taken by Frederick J. Breda

U.S. Library of Congress Cataloging in Publication Data

Silverstein, Alvin.
   Gerbils: all about them.

   Bibliography: p.
   Includes index.
   SUMMARY: Provides instructions for raising, training, and caring for gerbils. Includes a description of the characteristics and habitats of gerbils in their natural setting and in captivity as laboratory animals.
   1. Gerbils—Juvenile literature.   [1. Gerbils]   I. Silverstein, Virginia B., joint author.   II. Breda, Frederick.   III. Title.
QL737.R638S54   599'.3233   75-34390
ISBN-0-397-31660-7   ISBN-0-397-31661-5 (pbk.)

FOR JUNE AND BILL HARDENBURG

Acknowledgments

The authors would like to thank Frederick and Dorothy Breda and their son Fred for their enthusiastic support; Joe Haley, D. G. Robinson, Jr., and Delbert D. Thiessen for their kind help and interest in the project; Bob, Glenn, Carrie, Sharon, Laura, and Kevin for their patient cooperation; and especially Circe, Frisky, Sweetsie, Blimpo, Koko, Skippy, Harriet, Humphrey, and all the indulgent friends and acquaintances who provided homes for their numerous progeny.

Contents

About Gerbils

Perhaps you are one of the thousands of Americans who have a pet gerbil. Or if you do not have a gerbil of your own, it is likely that you know someone who owns a gerbil. But your parents probably did not have pet gerbils when they were young. Before 1954 there was not a single gerbil in the entire United States! And it was not until the 1960s that gerbils became widespread as pets.

The gerbils that are found in so many American homes and laboratories today are not native to the Western Hemisphere. They came originally from Mongolia, and they are related to other long-legged rodents that live wild in various parts of Asia, Europe, and Africa.

AN ASIAN IMMIGRANT

Nobody intended gerbils to become America's newest pet craze. What Dr. Victor Schwentker, the biologist who brought the first Mongolian gerbils to the United States, really wanted to do was to develop a new laboratory animal for scientific studies. Trained in genetics, the study of heredity, Dr. Schwentker gradually became more and more interested in laboratory animal science. Animals such as rats, mice, and guinea pigs are widely used in studies of how the organs of the body work in sickness and health, and in studies and tests of drugs. Such laboratory animals are similar to humans in many ways—similar enough so that studies of how they react to various conditions can provide valuable clues to how humans would react. But there are many differences between a mouse and a man, and scientists often find themselves wishing for better research animals—ones that would catch a particular disease, or use a certain vitamin more like people do.

Dr. Schwentker organized the West Foundation for research in laboratory animal science and began to explore the animal kingdom, hunting for overlooked animals that could be conveniently raised and studied in the laboratory. He studied tree shrews and pikas, lemmings, cotton rats, and Chinese hamsters. His laboratory at Tumblebrook Farm, in Brant Lake, New York, gradually grew into a leading commercial supplier of laboratory animals. And Tumblebrook Farm's greatest success was the gerbil.

Victor Schwentker was not the first scientist ever to raise and study gerbils. One of the first accounts of gerbil research appeared in 1892, in a book by Elie Metchnikoff, a Russian bacteriologist who later won a Nobel Prize for his work on the body's defenses against diseases. Metchnikoff used gerbils from Algeria to study resistance to tuberculosis. Later researchers used various species of gerbils from Europe, Asia, and Africa in their studies. But these experimenters all used wild gerbils, bought from local rodent-catchers. And these gerbils were not the species that eventually came to the United States. The trail from Mongolia to America in the gerbil's migration led through Japan.

Japanese researchers had been studying Mongolian gerbils since the 1930s. They had observed the animals in their

natural habitat, and then, starting with a shipment of twenty pairs in 1935, they launched an effort to develop gerbils as laboratory animals. Efforts to develop breeding stock were delayed by the war, but by 1949 there was a thriving colony of gerbils at the Central Laboratory for Experimental Animals in Japan. Researchers at the laboratory reported that not only were gerbils easy to raise, but they could be infected with many diseases that scientists were eager to study, such as tuberculosis, brucellosis, leprosy, and rabies. In America, Victor Schwentker read these reports with delight. It seemed that the Mongolian gerbil was exactly the animal he was looking for. It would be a valuable new animal for disease researchers to use and would also help to prove his point that many not so well known animals could make just as important a contribution to science as rats and mice.

Letters flew back and forth between Dr. Schwentker and a Japanese acquaintance, Michie Nomura, and arrangements were made. In 1954 a shipment arrived at Brant Lake. Eleven pairs of Mongolian gerbils had found a home on a new continent.

The months after the arrival of the gerbils were a busy time for the scientists and technicians at Tumblebrook Farm. Their Japanese colleagues had provided many helpful suggestions on gerbil raising, but they had to work out for themselves many of the details of the best ways to feed, house, and care for the new animals. In some ways gerbils are quite different from most other rodents, such as rats, mice, and hamsters. Rats and mice, for example, are usually caged with the sexes separated and are only brought together briefly for mating (often one male with several females). Hamsters must be caged separately and may fight viciously if they are left together. But gerbils are sociable little creatures, who not only like the company of other gerbils but mate for life. They are most content when they are housed together in pairs. With these unfamiliar details to work out—and with the gerbils recovering from the unsettling experience of a journey halfway around the world—Dr. Schwentker and his staff were not able to get all the gerbils to breed successfully. It turned out that just five females and four males were the parents of all the gerbils in the colony that became established at Tumble- brook Farm—and the ancestors of all the Mongolian gerbils living in the United States today.

While Dr. Schwentker and his staff were learning to care for gerbils and raising the first litters, an unexpected thing happened: They fell in love with the gerbils! An animal technician's work is often frustrating and depressing. He must clean and fill food and water containers every day, clean out smelly cages, and handle the animals each day so they will become tame and gentle. Many animals do not like to be handled at first. When a human appears, they tend to run and hide in the farthest corner of the cage, or they watch for an opportunity to dash out of an open cage door and scoot for the nearest crack in the woodwork. The technician who handles them may well be rewarded with a nasty bite or scratch. But caring for gerbils does not involve any of these troublesome experiences. The Tumblebrook Farm staff quickly nicknamed their new animals "gentle gerbils." When a gerbil's cage door is opened, it will usually scamper to the opening and look out curiously, sniffing with whiskers bristling. A person's hand is something to be explored, with a sniff of the nose and a gentle pat with a delicate front paw. It may even climb up onto the hand quite fearlessly. If a gerbil gets out of its cage, it doesn't try to escape. Instead, it meanders about exploring and soon either pops back into its cage or can be scooped up easily

A person's hand is something to be explored.

by the pursuing human. Caring for gerbils is easy, too. They were originally desert animals, and their bodies are built for conserving water. They drink very little water, excrete only a few drops of urine each day, and their droppings are small dry pellets. So cleaning a gerbil cage is a simple matter and need only be done every couple of weeks.

What happened next in the story of the gerbil in America has been described by a leading gerbil breeder as "unintentional and undesirable, but probably inevitable." Gerbil lovers would argue about how undesirable the result was, but certainly anyone who thought about it beforehand could have predicted what would happen. As soon as the gerbil colony was thriving and multiplying and there were plenty of "gentle gerbils" to spare, scientists and technicians began taking gerbils home with them for pets. Since two gerbils can begin breeding at about ten to twelve weeks of age and then can produce litters of up to a dozen every month or so, all year round, the families of these original gerbil owners soon had plenty of gerbils to give to eager friends and neighbors. The gerbils spread quickly through the country, both in scientific laboratories and as pets in people's homes. Pet shops began to stock them, and as gerbils became more plentiful their price dropped from about fifteen dollars a pair to about two or three dollars each.

Why would anyone be upset about the introduction of a new pet animal, especially one as appealing as the gerbil?

Scientists today tend to worry when an animal is taken from one part of the world and introduced into another. Sometimes the results are quite unexpected—and sometimes disastrous.

One thing that might go wrong is that a pet animal might carry diseases and transmit them to humans. Turtles, which used to be among the favorite pet animals, have recently been banned because it was found that they carry *Salmonella*, a bacterium that causes stomach upsets and other ailments. Fortunately Mongolian gerbils seem to be healthy little animals in general, and they don't seem to transmit any common diseases to people. Indeed, one test showed that although gerbils can be infected with a form of *Salmonella*, they just have a mild case of diarrhea for a few days and then recover completely. They do not become carriers of the disease.

Another problem scientists worry about when animals are moved from one part of the world to another is the possibility that they may get loose and live wild. No one is ever quite sure beforehand what the result may be. Animals that are pleasant and harmless in their native home may become pests when they are transplanted to a new region, where their usual natural enemies are not found. Gray squirrels taken from the United States to England have made a nuisance of themselves, and the less aggressive native red squirrels are disappearing from many areas. Sparrows and starlings, imported from England to the

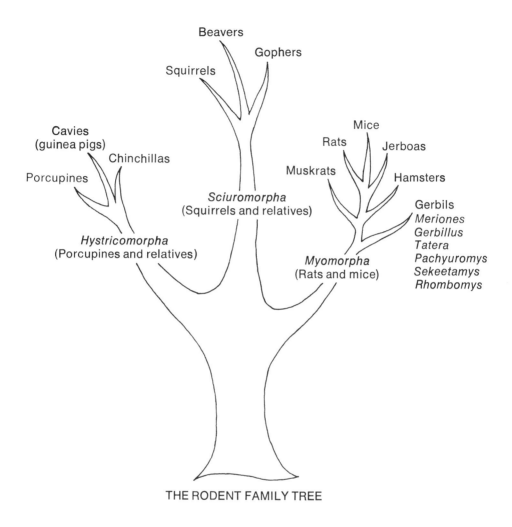

Beavers

Gophers

Squirrels

Mice

Rats

Jerboas

Cavies
(guinea pigs)

Chinchillas

Muskrats

Hamsters

Porcupines

Gerbils
*Meriones
Gerbillus
Tatera
Pachyuromys
Sekeetamys
Rhombomys*

Sciuromorpha
(Squirrels and relatives)

Hystricomorpha
(Porcupines and relatives)

Myomorpha
(Rats and mice)

THE RODENT FAMILY TREE

United States, have become so well established that they are pests in many areas. Newer threats are provided by some animals that were originally imported as pets and then escaped. Monk parakeets flew out of a broken crate in a New York airport and are now spreading through the Middle Atlantic States, damaging fruit crops. Walking catfish, piranhas, giant snails, and other exotic animals are threatening Florida and other southeastern states.

Ecologists believe that escaped gerbils probably would be kept in check by the same predators that feed on our native small rodents. But they are not sure, and they worry because some kinds of gerbils are pests in their native lands. Gerbils in India eat grain crops, and in the USSR gerbils undermine railroad embankments with their digging. In Africa, ratlike gerbils carry the dread bubonic plague. There are some regions in the United States where escaped gerbils might become established—particularly the hot, dry parts of the southwestern states. California has laws forbidding gerbils to be brought into the state.

MEET THE GERBIL

What is a gerbil? If you had to give a quick answer to that question after just looking at a gerbil or a picture of one, you would probably say that it's something like a large mouse or a small rat. And you would not be too far wrong. For gerbils (pronounced *JUR-bils*) belong to a large group of mouselike rodents.

There are more than two thousand kinds of rodents. Some of them are quite familiar animals. The large group of mouselike rodents, for example, includes not only gerbils, but also rats, mice, hamsters, and muskrats. Another group of rodents includes squirrels, gophers, and beavers. The third main group of rodents consists of the porcupines and their relatives. (Surprisingly, scientists include guinea pigs and chinchillas among the porcupine's closest relatives.)

Rodents belong to the class of mammals, animals which have a coat of fur or hair and which feed their young with milk. With a very few exceptions, rodents are small creatures. The small, sleek mouse scurrying into a corner, the squirrel with its bushy tail storing nuts in a hole high up in a tree trunk, the beaver building a dam, and the porcupine with its "armor" of sharp quills may seem quite different, both from one another and from a gerbil. But all the rodents share one main feature in common: all of them have four chisel-shaped front teeth (two upper and two lower) which are perfectly suited for gnawing.

A rodent's incisors are different from the front teeth of most other mammals. Once you lose your baby teeth and your permanent teeth grow in, they stop growing when they have reached a certain size. If you chip or break a permanent tooth, you will carry the evidence of your mishap for the rest of your life (unless a dentist repairs the damage). But a rodent's front teeth keep on growing throughout its life. Its ceaseless gnawing keeps its teeth worn down to a convenient size and keeps their cutting edges chisel-sharp. Much of the trouble that rats and mice cause when they are pests in people's houses is due to their

Chisellike front teeth.

constant need to gnaw, which drives them to chew up anything that is handy—books, rugs, even electric cables! Gnawing is really a life-and-death matter for a rodent: if it were kept in a cage with only soft foods to eat and nothing hard to gnaw on, its incisors would eventually grow so long that it would be unable to close its mouth. Unable to chew its food, it would starve.

Gerbils have the usual ever-growing rodent front teeth, plus a total of twelve molars (grinding teeth) toward the back of the jaws, separated from the incisors by a large gap on each side.

A full-grown gerbil is bigger than a mouse but smaller than a rat. It is about four inches long from nose to rump (plus another four inches for the tail) and weighs about three ounces. Its head is shorter and broader than a rat's. The gerbil has large dark eyes which bulge a bit, and very well-developed ears, which it holds erect. A gerbil's hind legs are considerably larger and stronger than its forelegs. It can sit up and stand on its hind legs easily, and it often does so, looking around like a miniature prairie dog or sitting up to eat. (Its forelegs are very nimble and can be used like hands to hold a seed or a chunk of food, or even to pick things up if the gerbil's mouth is already full.) A gerbil scurries about on all four legs. It usually runs with a jerky motion, interrupted by many stops to look around. Those long, strong hind legs look like good jumping legs, and

Bigger than a mouse, smaller than a rat.

Large, dark eyes.

A gerbil can sit up and stand on its hind legs easily.

indeed they are. When a gerbil is frightened, in a hurry, or just feeling frisky, it can leap straight up in the air or forward, backward, or sideways, covering up to several feet in a single bound. Each hind foot has five toes, equipped with long black claws. (Another name for the Mongolian gerbil is the "clawed jird.") A gerbil's forefoot also has five toes, but the "thumb" is small and clawless and looks only half-finished.

The gerbil uses its hind feet for something else besides sitting up and moving about: foot-stomping. Sometimes a sort of knocking or drumming sound can be heard as a gerbil rhythmically stamps on the ground with its hind feet. Scientists who have studied gerbils have a number of ideas about what this foot-stomping means, but so far they are not sure. Sometimes the stomping seems to signal an alert to other gerbils—perhaps a warning of danger or a signal that food is available. Sometimes a gerbil seems to be stamping because it is annoyed, like a child throwing a temper tantrum. Foot-stomping often occurs during mating, which for gerbils is a rather long-drawn-out affair. The male wildly chases the female around and around in a circle, until she suddenly stops and lets him catch her. He mounts her briefly, and then they break away to wash themselves, licking their fur with their tongues like house cats. Then the restless male begins a rhythmic foot-stomping. (Less often the female may stomp too.) Soon they are

Claws on "fingers" and toes.

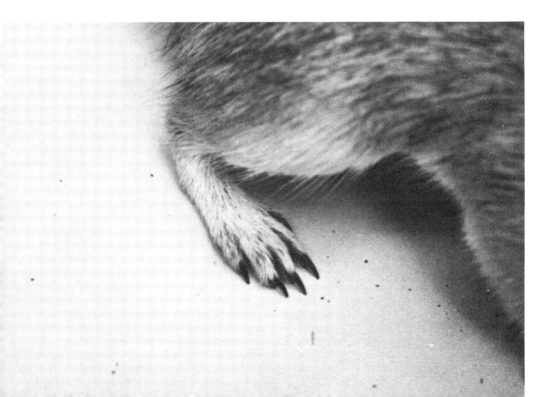

up and dashing about again in another chase. They may go on for hours, pausing now and then to rest.

A gerbil is covered with fur from the tip of its nose to the end of its tail—even the soles of its feet are hairy. The body fur of a gerbil is very thick and soft. The fur on its back is a tawny brown, but it is not a solid color—more a "tweedy" effect. When the fur is ruffled, it can be seen that about half of each hair (the part closest to the body) is black, and the hairs are also black-tipped. The fur on a gerbil's underparts is much lighter—a creamy tan. These hairs are not black-tipped, but they do have a black portion close to the body. Unlike the bare, scaly tail of a rat, a gerbil's tail is completely covered with hair. A tuft of longer black-tipped hairs at the end of the tail makes it look rather like a lion's tail. The gerbil, like its cousin the rat, uses its tail for balance, but it does not usually curl its tail around things, as a rat or mouse does. When a gerbil runs, it often holds its

A long tail helps the gerbil keep its balance.

tail straight out behind it, like a banner. When it sits up on its haunches, the tail acts as a prop.

The gerbil's fur coat provides good camouflage in the sandy, rocky lands of its native home. If by chance a wild gerbil in Mongolia were born with white fur or black fur, it would stand out sharply against the bare, sandy soil. Predators such as hawks and foxes would be able to spot it more easily than its normally colored brothers and sisters. Very likely it would end up as a predator's meal while it was still young, before it had a chance to mate and pass on its new trait to young of its own.

But when animals are raised in captivity, protective

A gerbil's fur coat is good camouflage.

coloring does not provide any particular advantage, since humans furnish protection from predators. And animal breeders are quick to pick out any unusual or interesting-looking animals to be the parents of new stock. Wild house mice, for example, have short, straight fur that is either gray or brown. But today nearly every pet shop stocks mice in a wide variety of colors—pure white mice with ruby-red eyes, black mice, cinnamon-colored mice, spotted mice. Curly-haired mice and nearly hairless mice have also been bred. Golden hamsters have been bred in captivity only since 1930, but already white-banded, spotted, albino (pure white), cream-colored, gray, and other varieties are available.

When gerbils were introduced into the United States, gerbil breeders examined each new litter carefully for mutations, sudden hereditary changes in color or shape or other traits. Most scientists and breeders expected that one of the first mutations would be an albino variation, with a white coat and red eyes. Such mutations are rather common throughout the animal kingdom. There are albino rats and mice, albino porcupines, cats, people—even albino birds and fish have been found. An albino's body lacks the ability to make the dark brown pigment melanin, which normally colors hair, eyes, and skin. Geneticists call albinism a recessive trait, by which they mean that it shows up only if an animal has inherited it from both parents. (Traits that show their effects even when they are inherited from only one parent are called dominant traits.) Dr. Schwentker's gerbil colony contained the descendants of just nine original parents, and in the course of breeding the animals there were many brother-and-sister or cousin matings. Many of the baby gerbils received just about the same heredity from both mother and father, so it was quite likely that once genetic changes had occurred, sooner or later they would show up even if they were recessive.

Gerbil breeders watched and waited for the first mutations. But for about fifteen years there was nothing. And when mutations finally did appear, they were not albinos. So far not a single albino Mongolian gerbil has been reported, anywhere in the world.

The first gerbil mutant showed up in the stock of a commercial breeder, Petersen Hamstery, in Burlington, North Carolina. It was a gerbil with white spots. Some of its descendants had white spots, too. And when suitable matings were arranged, a group of spotted gerbils was gradually obtained. In 1969 the spot mutant was turned over to another animal breeder, Haley Farm, in Virginia, for development. The owner, Joe Haley, and his staff worked with the new mutation, investigating how it was inherited and what further variations might be developed. The new mutation is a dominant trait, and for a while each successive generation had more white than its ancestors. The breeders hoped that their new gerbil stock might eventually produce pure white animals. But the new color

28

Some of the spot mutants have nearly perfect "Dutch belted" markings.

trait stabilized as a sort of piebald spotting. Another interesting thing about it is that it seems to be influenced by the sex of the animal. Although both male and female gerbils can show the spotting, it is more prominent in males. In the same litter, the males usually have about twice as much white on their coats as their sisters have.

The next color mutation turned up in the early 1970s. This was a recessive mutation in which the gerbil's coat is nearly all black, with a small white stripe on the neck and foreparts.

Developing a new variety of gerbils is a rewarding and exciting task, but it can be a chancy and frustrating business, too. The first black gerbil was born in the first litter of a pair of young gerbils owned by an air force sergeant, Norman W. Olsen. It was a male, and when the original pair produced another litter, about thirty days later, another black male was born. Sergeant Olsen managed to get one of the black males to breed with its mother, and two litters yielded equal numbers of black and brown males—but no females at all! Finally, in the third litter of the black male and its agouti (brown) mother, there were three black females and one black male.

When all the black gerbils (a total of three females and five males) were full grown, they were housed together in a large cage, and Sergeant Olsen eagerly waited for litters of black gerbils to appear. But for a year nothing happened. The gerbils did not breed. Sergeant Olsen wrote to D. G. Robinson, Jr., of Tumblebrook Farm for advice. He then

The black mutant has a little white on its face and forepaws.

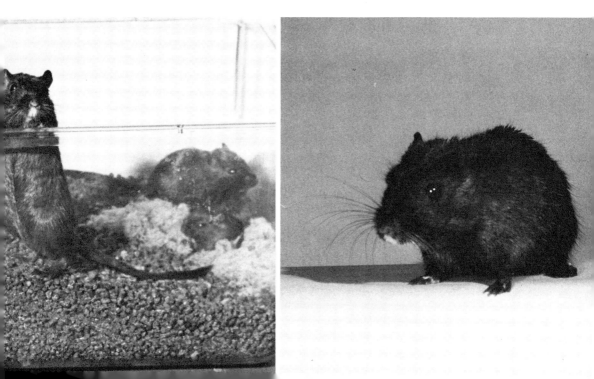

tried pairing off the three black females with three of the black males and moving each pair to an individual cage. In about four months, each pair produced a litter. But the parents seemed nervous in their new quarters, and killed all the young. The same thing happened to the next litter!

Sergeant Olsen was getting worried. The black gerbils were more than a year and a half old and nearing the end of their reproductive period. If they did not succeed in raising a new generation of young, the new line of black gerbils would die out. Finally, moving the gerbils to a quiet environment with a constant temperature brought success, and new litters were born, raised, and weaned.

Meanwhile, D. G. Robinson, Jr., advised Sergeant Olsen on how to develop the black gerbils for use in research. Eventually Sergeant Olsen coauthored a scientific paper on the use of black gerbils in cancer studies, which was published in the journal *Laboratory Animal Science* in 1974. Some of the black gerbils were also sent to Tumble-brook Farm, where the variety is being developed for distribution.

So far, these are the only two mutations that have been reported in gerbils. But scientists are confident that it will be only a matter of time before others appear. Meanwhile, it will be interesting to see what new variations will result when the spot mutant and the black mutant are more widely available and are bred to each other.

LIFE IN THE DESERT

The gerbils that are so widespread in the United States today originally came from the Gobi Desert regions of Mongolia and northeastern China. They were first described back in 1811, by a naturalist named J. K. Illiger. They did not receive an official, scientific name until 1867, when the naturalist A. Milne-Edwards gave them the name *Meriones unguiculatus*. *Meriones* comes from a Persian myth; it was the name of a warrior-god who wore a battle helmet decorated with boar tusks. *Unguiculatus* is a Latin word meaning "clawed." What a fierce-sounding name for such a gentle, friendly little animal!

Many of the regions where gerbils are found in their native land are rather sparsely inhabited and difficult to get

The Mongolian gerbil was originally a desert animal.

to. As a result, not all the details of their normal daily life are known. But some field observations have been made, and the behavior of gerbils in captivity offers some clues. Recently some experiments being conducted at the University of Texas at Austin, in which gerbils are observed in a recreated "natural" habitat, have brought some interesting new insights.

Mongolian gerbils normally live in dry regions with a loose sandy soil, dotted here and there with sparse vegetation. They live in underground communities, digging tunnels about six to eight feet long, with perhaps half a dozen entrances, a number of branch tunnels at different levels, and chambers that are used for nesting and food storage. The large round nesting chamber is lined with grasses and leaves, chewed and shredded to make a soft bedding. A gerbil digs in much the same way as a dog. The forepaws do most of the work, scraping at the soil. Periodically the gerbil stops and kicks the accumulated dirt away behind it with its hind feet. Sometimes it uses its head as a battering ram, pushing through the loose soil nose first. (When you hold a gerbil in your hand, you may notice it butting and shoving with its muzzle against the gaps between your fingers.) Shifting sands, blown by the winds or moved by the gerbils themselves, plug the entrances to the burrows, so that it is difficult for the gerbils' enemies to find them. The plugs also help to conserve moisture and keep an even temperature inside the burrow.

A desert is a place of great temperature extremes. During the day it is blazing hot, while at night it may be chilling cold. Like many other desert animals, gerbils get some relief from temperature extremes by remaining in their burrows during the hottest part of the day and the coldest part of the night. But these small desert dwellers are far more adaptable to wide temperature swings than most other animals. In experiments it has been found that they can endure temperatures up to 110°F for as long as five hours. If they have enough bedding to snuggle into, they can survive temperatures below 0°F. Thanks to this adaptability, gerbils can be active both day and night, all year round, despite the burning heat of the summer and the freezing nights of the winter. They pop in and out of their burrows, scurry along the ground gathering food, and sometimes sit on their haunches just outside the entrances to their burrows like tiny prairie dogs.

One of the most important aspects of the desert environment is the lack of water. Gerbils are marvelously adapted to life in arid lands. Though they will drink water if it is available, they can get along quite well without any drinking water at all. They get all the moisture they need from the tender young leaves of grasses that they eat in the spring and summer—or even from the dry seeds and grains on which they feed in the fall and winter. In a gerbil's body fats are oxidized to provide water and energy. If a gerbil has no drinking water, its blood gets a little thicker than usual but still flows freely enough through the blood vessels of its body. Exceptionally efficient kidneys permit the gerbil to conserve precious water. These organs absorb most of the water in the gerbil's wastes, so that it excretes only a drop or two of very concentrated urine each day. Food wastes, too, are concentrated as they pass through the gerbil's digestive system, so that they emerge as small dry pellets.

From April to August, when fresh food is plentiful, the gerbils' storerooms are empty. But as autumn approaches, they begin to store away grains for the winter. As much as four or five pounds of seeds and grains are stored in one burrow. With this ample food supply, and protection from the cold weather, the gerbils stay active through the winter. They do not hibernate, as do many other animals, such as groundhogs and hamsters.

Not only are gerbils active all year round, but they mate all year round as well, with no special mating season. At about eight or ten weeks of age, the gerbils begin to pair off. They are ready to mate at about ten to twelve weeks, and the young are born about twenty-four days after mating. The size of the litter varies from as few as one to as many as a dozen; the average is about four. Usually young mothers have larger litters. The female gerbil is ready to mate again immediately after she has given birth, which means that by the time her young ones are ready to be weaned she has a new litter arriving. If she is nursing a

35

particularly large litter, an unusual thing happens. The tiny babies forming inside her body stop developing and just wait in a sort of suspended animation. When the nursing young begin to eat solid food, the new babies pick up where they left off, finish their development inside their mother's body, and are born—a couple of weeks late! Female gerbils usually have several litters in a year, but they generally stop bearing young at about fourteen months.

When a baby gerbil is born, it doesn't look much like a gerbil. It is pink and hairless, its nose is blunt, its eyes and ears are sealed tight shut, and its tail is a stubby little thing, only a quarter of the length of its body. But it grows quickly, fed by its mother's milk, and by three to four

Newborn gerbils are completely hairless.

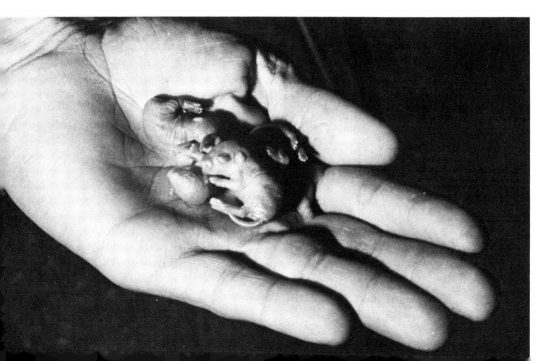

weeks it is ready to be weaned. If a new litter has not arrived, the mother may continue to nurse her young for up to six weeks.

The young gerbils may remain with their parents, enlarging the colony's burrow. Or they may leave to dig new burrows of their own. Delbert Thiessen at the University of Texas has been studying gerbils under conditions similar to their natural habitat and has found that the males tend to stake out and defend a home territory. If a strange gerbil tries to enter the territory, the resident male attacks, boxing and kicking the intruder until he is driven away. The gerbil marks his territory with an oily substance, produced in a special scent gland on the underside of his belly. He marks stones and other objects around his boundaries by rubbing his belly over them. The

female gerbil also has a scent gland, although it is somewhat smaller than the male's. Normally she does not do as much scent marking, except when she is nursing a litter of young. At that time her scent gland is enlarged and she is very active and aggressive, ready to defend her babies against intruders.

Many of the most striking features of a gerbil's body are successful adaptations to desert life. Its well-developed ears pick up the faintest sounds carrying over the desert. The hairy soles of its feet insulate them from the hot sand as it scurries about. And its strong hind legs equip it for leaping, the most economical method of moving about in search of scarce food in the arid lands. A gerbil's agile leaps are also its main defense against enemies such as eagles and hawks, snakes and foxes. Its sleek, slippery fur is hard to get a firm hold on, and before the predator has realized its prey is slipping away, a gerbil can leap in any direction—forward, backward, sideways, straight up in the air—zigzagging, or even turning around in midair. The young gerbils, in particular, make up for their inexperience by an instinctive skittishness. The slightest noise or motion will "spook" them, and they go leaping away madly in all directions like popcorn out of a popper.

That the gerbil's life-style is a highly successful adaptation to desert conditions is underlined by the fact that two other groups of desert rodents that are not very closely related to gerbils look and act amazingly like them. One group is the jerboas, which live in Asia and northern Africa.

This detail from an ancient Persian tapestry shows gerbillike rodents.

The other includes the kangaroo rats of the southwestern United States. Both jerboas and kangaroo rats leap about on the same kind of kangaroolike hind legs as the gerbil has. Both balance themselves with the aid of a long tail with a tuft of fur at the tip. Like the gerbil, they have large, well-developed ears, and hairy soles on their feet. They can live on a diet of dry seeds, without any drinking water, and they live in burrows which they keep plugged during the heat of the day. The resemblance between gerbils and jerboas is so great that it gave the gerbil its common name: "gerbil" comes from the Latin *gerbillus*, which literally means "little jerboa."

The gerbil, jerboa, and kangaroo rat independently developed strikingly similar adaptations to desert life.

OTHER KINDS OF GERBILS

Gerbils, jerboas, and kangaroo rats are all related to some degree, since all are members of the group of mouselike rodents. But the Mongolian gerbils have a number of far closer relatives, belonging to what scientists refer to as the Subfamily Gerbillinae. About a hundred different species of gerbils are known, including fourteen different kinds of *Meriones*. One of the largest groups (about forty species) consists of the "sand rats," whose scientific name is *Gerbillus*.

The sand rats, such as *Gerbillus gerbillus*, are among the most common of the small mammals found in desert or near-desert regions of Africa and Asia. They are usually more slenderly built than the Mongolian gerbils, with long kangaroolike hind legs, large ears, and a tail that is considerably longer than the gerbil's body. The fur on the back is a tawny color, or mousy gray, or reddish brown, depending on the species, while the fur on the underparts is usually white or cream-colored. These gerbils are sociable little animals and often dig their burrows in the sand so

The sand rat is more slender than the Mongolian gerbil.

close together that they form colonies. They are active mainly in the nighttime, keeping to their burrows during the heat of the desert day. It is said that they are attracted to campfires and hop up and down at the edge of the ring of light.

The naked-soled gerbils, found in Asia and Africa, are not desert animals. They live in plains or woodlands; sometimes they are pests in cultivated fields and gardens. As you can guess from their name, the soles of their feet are not hairy, although they look like typical gerbils otherwise. (They do not need protection from hot desert sands.) The naked-soled gerbils that live in India, *Tatera indica,* dig two kinds of burrows: short bolt-holes for sudden escapes from danger, and deeper burrows for living quarters. The deeper burrows have so many tunnels, entrances, and exits that they are like an underground maze. The nest chamber is in the center of the maze, and the entrances are usually blocked with dirt. These gerbils feed mainly on green

The naked-soled gerbil is not a desert rodent.

plants, seeds, bulbs, and roots, but they like to vary their diet with a bit of meat, eating eggs and young birds whenever they can. The naked-soled gerbils that live in Africa are considered a danger to health, for their fleas may carry the germs of the dread bubonic plague.

Fat-tailed gerbils, *Pachyuromys duprasi*, are found in sandy regions of northern Africa. They are stocky little animals, with soft, light-colored fur. Their name comes from their unusual tail: it is short, thick, and club-shaped, and completely covered with fur.

It is easy to see how the fat-tailed gerbil got its name.

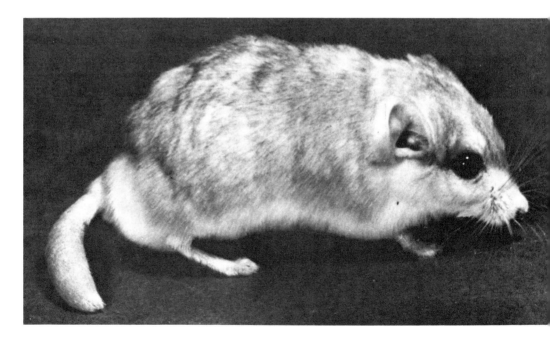

The bushy-tailed jird puzzled scientists for a while.

The bushy-tailed jird, *Sekeetamys calurus,* carries the typical tuft at the end of the tail to an extreme—the large white tuft at the end of its tail looks almost like a whisk broom. This gerbil lives in deserts and rocky slopes of Palestine, Sinai, and eastern Egypt. It burrows under boulders and rock ledges and climbs nimbly over the rocks in its home. (Its feet are naked-soled.) Scientists have been puzzled about where to put the bushy-tailed jird in their classification of gerbils. First it was assigned to the *Gerbillus* group. Then it seemed to fit better with the *Meriones.* Finally it was decided that it is different enough from other gerbils to have a genus of its own, *Sekeetamys.* Studies of chromosomes, the tiny units of heredity that are found in each cell of an animal's body, helped to clinch this decision.

The largest of all the gerbils is the great gerbil, *Rhombomys opimus,* which is found in deserts and foothills of Iran, Afghanistan, the eastern part of the USSR, China, and Mongolia. It is a stocky animal, up to eight inches long from nose to rump, with a tail about four-fifths the length of its body. Great gerbils are active mainly during the day, all year round. But in regions where snow is heaped high through much of the winter, the great gerbils mostly keep to their burrows. Only a few entrances and air holes are kept open through the snow. The gerbils are snug inside, with up to a hundred pounds of food that they have stored away for the winter. In the USSR the great gerbils are pests, damaging crops, railway embankments, and the sides of irrigation channels. But in some areas they are trapped for their thick, soft fur.

Gerbils as Pets

Are you looking for a pet that is lively but gentle, clean, easy to feed and care for, and doesn't take up much room? Like millions of other pet owners, you will find just what you are looking for in a gerbil—or better yet, two!

CHOOSING A GERBIL

Before you pick out pet gerbils—from a pet shop or a litter raised by a friend—you have an important decision to make: How many gerbils do you want? A single gerbil can live well enough, particularly if you give it plenty of love and attention and a wealth of interesting things to play with. But scientists and pet raisers have found that gerbils are rather sociable animals. They are most active and seem to be most contented when they are living together in pairs. They can even be raised together peacefully in larger groups, of up to fifty, as long as the cage area is large

enough and the gerbils have known one another since they were very young.

Having gerbils in pairs can present some problems, though. Gerbils can begin breeding as early as ten weeks old, and if conditions are ideal they can produce a litter nearly every month for more than a year after that! Of course, it is fun to watch gerbils raise their families, as Mama and Papa take turns with the baby-sitting chores. But since an average litter size is more than four, and since baby gerbils quickly grow up to have litters of their own, you can rapidly find yourself swamped with more gerbils than anyone but a commercial gerbil breeder would know what to do with.

If you would like the fun of having gerbils without the responsibility of a gerbil population explosion, there are some solutions to the problem. Two males or two females from the same litter can live together quite peaceably. (Unrelated animals of the same sex may fight unless they have been raised together from an early age—just after weaning.) Or you might find an older pair of gerbils, past the breeding age, perfect for you. Gerbils usually stop breeding after about a year and a half, but they can live up to five years or even longer, so there's plenty of time for fun without having to worry about gerbil birth control. Or you might be able to obtain a younger pair of gerbils who are unable to breed for some reason. (For example, after a number of generations of inbreeding—matings within the

Gerbils can multiply quickly.

same close family group—female gerbils develop tumors in their ovaries and are unable to have young.) You could consult with the pet shop owner and possibly have a pair ordered specially.

Pet shops normally carry fairly young gerbils, perhaps six to eight weeks old. They may have whole litters or may sell gerbils in mated pairs. (One pet shop in our area had to keep the same pair of gerbils on display for three straight months. According to local humane society regulations, the shop was not allowed to sell gerbils if the female was pregnant or nursing a litter. This particular pair of gerbils mated right after they arrived at the pet shop, had their litter, then had another litter as soon as that one was weaned, and another one after that. Every time we visited the pet shop, there was the same pair of gerbils in a cage with a NOT FOR SALE sign. Finally a customer managed to catch them between pregnancies and bought them.)

If you want to breed gerbils and have the fun of watching them raise their young, it is best to get a male and a female that are not closely related. And, if possible, introduce them to each other while they are still young, before they are sexually mature. (About eight or nine weeks old is best.) Arranging a gerbil "wedding" is a great responsibility. Unlike most rodents, gerbils seem to be naturally monogamous—they choose a single mate, remain together, share in the rearing of the young, and remain faithful for life. Indeed, a gerbil "widow" may refuse to take another mate.

Telling the sex of gerbils is fairly easy, especially if you have a number of animals of both sexes to compare. The key is the gerbil's hindquarters. A female gerbil's rump is short and rounded, and on the underside of her body the anal and genital openings are very close together. A male gerbil has a tapered bulge near the base of his tail, with a dark-colored scrotal pouch that sometimes bulges out prominently and at times is smaller and partly hidden by tufts of fur. His anal and genital openings are quite far apart. In general, male gerbils tend to be larger and heavier

It's easy to tell male and female gerbils apart. The female is on the left, and the male is on the right.

than females of the same age, but the size difference is not as sure a method of telling them apart.

In choosing your gerbils, you will want to start out with healthy, active animals. Watch what happens when the cage is opened. Gerbils are so inquisitive that they will normally come scampering over to investigate, sniffing at the salesperson's hand and leaning out to look around. If they haven't been handled very much, they may quickly take fright and scamper away. But soon their curiosity overcomes them, and they are back again to investigate.

A healthy gerbil's body is firm-looking. Extreme fatness may be a sign of overeating (or a diet too high in fats), or it may indicate old age, since gerbils tend to get heavy when

A healthy gerbil will come running over to investigate as soon as the cage is opened.

they are old. The gerbil's eyes should be large, dark, and bright. Its fur should be long and soft, with a sleek, smooth appearance. If a gerbil has just been washing itself, or if it has just gotten up from a nap in a heap of other gerbils, its fur may be somewhat ruffled, but it will smooth down in a few minutes. Watch out for bare spots. Bald spots near the base of the tail are usually a sign of overcrowding—when too many gerbils are together in one cage, they sometimes nibble nervously at one another's tails. The fur will quickly grow back on such spots when the gerbils are moved to a new cage with plenty of room. A bare spot on a gerbil's nose may be caused by rubbing against the wires of a cage, or it may be a sign of a dietary deficiency or of some more serious condition. It's better not to take a chance on a gerbil like that.

Until now, prospective gerbil owners have not had any choice of fur color. All the gerbils for sale in pet shops have had the same agouti or wild-type coat, with black-tipped reddish or tawny brown fur on the back and light gray or creamy fur on the underparts. The agouti gerbil is an attractive little animal, but variety is always interesting, and gerbils with different coat colors or markings would be easier to tell apart at a glance. Fortunately, the spot mutant and black mutant gerbils are now ready for general distribution. Such "fancy" gerbils should quickly become popular in pet shops all across the country, and in time it is likely that other mutants will appear. Indeed, your own gerbils might give birth to a mutant that has never been seen before. (If you suspect that you have a new variety of gerbil, it would be a good idea to write to an established breeder such as Tumblebrook Farm for advice on how to develop it.)

HOUSING

Before you bring your new gerbils home, you must arrange for a secure place to keep them. We know of some people who have given gerbils the free run of the house, allowing them to go where they please and just return to their cage to eat and sleep. We don't advise this, for a number of reasons. First of all, gerbils on the loose might too easily get hurt. They are small and tend to get underfoot, so they can easily be stepped on. Cats or dogs may catch them. In addition, there are too many things around a house for a gerbil to get into and do damage. Its constantly gnawing rodent teeth can chew up papers, clothes, and rugs. Even worse, it may bite into electric wires and cause a short circuit or even a fire.

You can't keep gerbils in a cardboard box. They would quickly chew right through the cardboard. If the sides of the box were low enough, the gerbils would simply jump out.

The wire cages made for small animals are generally fine for a gerbil, as long as the spaces between the bars or mesh are small enough (about a quarter of an inch). A gerbil can stretch its body and squeeze through a far smaller gap than you'd ever suspect. And gerbil babies are so tiny and active that they could easily slip through the bars of a birdcage, for example, and fall out. A gerbil can't gnaw its way out of a wire cage, and climbing up and down the walls of the cage will provide some extra exercise for it. (A gerbil's feet are not built properly for walking upside down on the roof of the cage as a rat or mouse can, though.) But one problem with a metal wire cage is that the gerbils will chew on the wires, making an annoying noise and risking a broken tooth.

In recent years a number of plastic cages specially designed for hamsters and gerbils have come on the market.

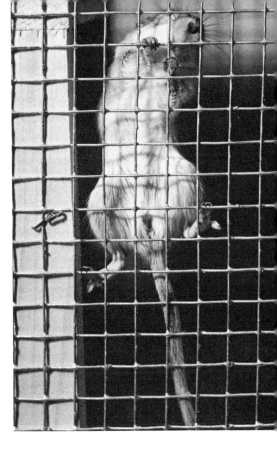

Climbing a wire cage
can provide exercise.

A gerbil could chew right through plastic, but the cages are designed so that there are no unprotected plastic edges it could get started on, so there is no danger of pet gerbils eating their way out of the plastic cages.

We have been using a group of Habitrail cages for our gerbils for about a year and have found they have a number of advantages, as well as some disadvantages. They are attractive, with clear plastic walls that give a continuous view of the gerbils' antics. They are compact, and the wire mesh floor with snap-out tray underneath makes them fairly easy to clean. The variety of connecting tunnels available

Wire cages . . .

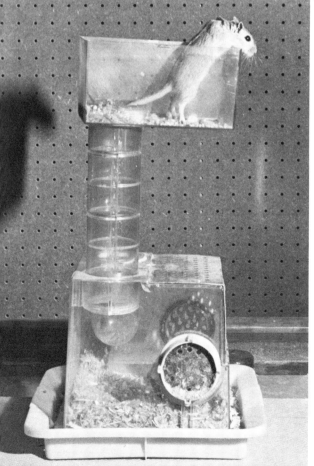

and plastic cages.

makes it possible to build up an interesting and homelike environment for a group of gerbils. But the snap-together connections do not come apart very readily, which makes it more difficult to clean the individual cage units in a complicated setup.

When we first looked into the idea of plastic cages, we suspected that there might not be enough ventilation and that things would tend to get damp and moldy inside the cage. We have found no such problems; apparently the air holes provide enough air circulation to keep the cages comfortable. We did have trouble with the water bottles that came with the cages. Every one that we tried (including a replacement sent by the manufacturer) began to leak, either immediately or suddenly after a day or so. We finally had to give up and remove the water dispensers, supplying our gerbils with moisture through regular rations of lettuce. We also found such frills as a plastic exercise pan and a "curiosity cube" clever but impractical. The gerbils seemed to enjoy running on them and popping in and out of the windows and doors of the cube, but they enjoyed even more chewing on the edges of the plastic. This activity not only rapidly wrecked the play devices, but also produced a horrible rasping noise that reverberated through the house and threatened to drive us all crazy. After a few days, we removed the exercise pan and cube from the cages and saved them for the times we took our gerbils out for a supervised run on a tabletop or counter.

The "curiosity cube" was fun, but the gerbils chewed away the doorway.

The main disadvantage of the plastic cages, though, is their high cost, especially considering the amount of space they provide for the money. The standard-size plastic cage, which runs close to ten dollars in most stores, is only about seven inches square. This is a little on the small side, although we have found that a pair of gerbils seems healthy and content in the "starter set" (a standard-size cage, plus a six-by-three-inch "sky house," connected to the main cage by a climbable tunnel, which the gerbils seem to enjoy using). Dr. Victor Schwentker recommends about eighteen square inches of floor space for each gerbil at three weeks of age, gradually increasing to thirty-six square inches for a mature gerbil—so the sixty-seven square inches provided by a Habitrail cage with sky house is about right for a pair of gerbils. But if the pair is raising a litter, they will need more room than a single cage can provide, and it is necessary to add on one or more "spare rooms."

The most convenient and inexpensive way we have found to house gerbils is a glass fish tank. It is roomy, easy to clean, and provides a real "picture window" view of the gerbils' world. A small crack in one of the walls, which would ruin the tank as an aquarium, presents no problem in keeping gerbils. Sometimes a pet shop will be willing to sell leaky fish tanks at a reduced price. (Many pet shops find that fish tanks are the most convenient and vivid way to display their gerbils and other small animals.)

If you use a fish tank for gerbils, you must have a wire mesh cover for it. (Never use a slab of glass for the top, as it will cut off all the fresh air.) When we transferred a litter of month-old gerbils to a ten-by-twenty-inch fish tank, we didn't happen to have any wire mesh handy. We used a piece of one-inch mesh chicken wire as a temporary cover, wondering whether a cover was really necessary, other than to protect the gerbils from our cats. From time to time we noticed the little gerbils jumping up, but they never seemed to get very close to the top. Then we read in a pet manual that gerbils can jump only six inches vertically; since the fish tank was more than twelve inches high, we figured it was safe enough. But our gerbils didn't read the book—and they faithfully practiced their high jumps. Fortunately we happened to be in the room when one of them, bouncing

A fish tank is great for gerbil watching. But it needs a gerbil-proof cover. (They slipped right through that chicken wire.)

up and down like a rubber ball, finally made it to the top, gracefully slipped out through the chicken wire mesh, scampered over it to the edge, and dropped down to the countertop below. No sooner was she replaced in the tank than she was at it again. Then followed a frantic hunt through the cellar and garage for an old screen we could cut up for a proper wire mesh top—which had turned out to be very necessary after all!

A gerbil's needs for cage furnishings are very simple and easy to supply. First of all, there should be a layer of litter in the bottom of the cage, mainly to catch the gerbils' droppings and the few drops of urine they produce each day. Wood shavings or chips, ground corncobs, sand, hay, leaves, shredded paper, and commercial litters are all quite satisfactory. The gerbils will chew up some of this material for bedding, shredding it fine. It is amusing to watch a gerbil chew on a piece of paper. It works along the edge, making a row of tiny punches with its teeth, until the paper shreds away in a fine strip. In their spare time, the gerbils may also work on other materials, such as the discarded shells of sunflower seeds, shredding them into fine slivers to add to the bedding. They also appreciate softer materials, such as strips of facial tissues. (A friend suggested absorbent cotton, but we found that it quickly gets unpleasantly dirty and messy-looking.)

Plenty of litter . . . and a place to call home.

Their eyes aren't even open yet, and they already know how to shred the wood shavings.

The gerbils frequently rearrange their bedding, sometimes according to the temperature and sometimes apparently just by whim. (We still haven't figured out why one group of our gerbils, housed in two connected cages, regularly moves their bedding every week or so—first into the left-hand cage, then back into the right one, and then into the left one again.) If it is very warm in the room, the gerbils will usually trample their bedding down and sleep on top of it. In somewhat cooler weather, they will gather it up into a cozy nest. If it is quite cool, they fluff up the bedding materials so that they fill the entire cage.

You may notice that your gerbils are fairly neat house-keepers. If you have a group of connected cages, the gerbils will place all of their bedding in just one compartment, which they will use as a nesting chamber, as wild gerbils do in their underground burrows. Into another compartment they will carry or drag sticks, nut shells, extra food pellets, and anything else that seems interesting or useful. (The gerbils will also hide bits of food among the bedding in the nesting chamber, handy for midnight snacks.) Usually gerbils will select one corner of the cage, or one compartment, in which to leave nearly all of their droppings. The gerbils' home does not stay quite as clean as it might, though, for these rodents are constantly scratching up the litter and bedding materials and rearranging them, so that everything regularly gets pretty well mixed up. But you can usually tell where their "bathroom" corner is when you clean the cage.

The gerbils' desert ancestry has made things very convenient for the gerbil owner. Since their droppings are almost completely dry and they produce very little urine, the cage stays dry and nearly odorless. Cage cleaning is usually a simple matter of dumping out the old litter (if you have a garden, it will make good compost) and wiping down the cage with a damp cloth or a disinfectant solution. Be sure the cage is dry before you put the new litter and the gerbils in.

The cage need be cleaned no oftener than every two

weeks or so. In fact, scientists have discovered a reason why gerbil cages should not be cleaned too frequently. Gerbils, like some other animals, have the habit of eating part of their droppings. This may seem like a rather unpleasant habit to humans, but it has a practical value for the gerbils. Bacteria that live in their intestines produce valuable vitamins, especially B vitamins. Some of these vitamins pass out of the gerbils' bodies with their droppings, but they recapture them by eating the droppings. When gerbils are raised in a cage with a wire mesh floor, through which droppings fall, it is recommended that they be given a vitamin-enriched feed. (In practice, droppings lost through the mesh floor may not be such a serious problem; we have noticed our gerbils reaching down through the mesh and pulling up dropped food, litter, and other materials from the tray beneath.)

Devices for supplying food and water are frequently provided in animal cages. Gerbils do not really need a food container. If a dish or bowl is placed inside the cage, the gerbils will just chew on it, knock it over, and dump bedding into it—and will probably drag their food away to eat it somewhere else anyway. Commercial cages some-times have automatic dispensing feeders. But for the average person with only a few gerbil pets, it is just as easy to deposit the feed on the floor of the cage. Water should never be provided in an open dish. The gerbils will quickly foul it with bedding materials, and if a mother gerbil is

A water bottle with a bent tube is best.

raising a litter, the babies might blunder into the dish and drown. A water bottle with a metal spout usually works best. Some cages have a built-in slot for one to fit into; or a bottle can be wired onto the side of a wire cage or suspended with wires from the corner of a fish tank. You will find that the gerbils do not use up their water very quickly; they drink only a few drops each day. Be sure to set up the water bottle so that it is not in contact with any bedding materials, which would act as a wick and drain the water out of the bottle. And never leave a leaking water bottle in a gerbil cage. Wet bedding can be very unpleasant and unhealthful for an animal, particularly for a desert animal like a gerbil.

If you wish, you can dispense with a water bottle entirely and simply give the gerbils lettuce two or three times a week. Our gerbils have done quite nicely that way and often do not seem very interested in water even if it is offered. An important exception is when a pair of gerbils is raising a litter. We have been keeping our gerbils in the bathroom, in cages on the countertop and on a broad windowsill (out of direct sunlight, which can make it too hot inside the cage). We got into the habit of letting two of the gerbils, Circe and Frisky, run about on the countertop several times a day. Then Circe had her first litter, and we suddenly discovered that as soon as she and Frisky were released from the cage, they would run over to the washbasin, jump down, and lap up any stray drops of water that had splashed from the faucet. They quickly trained us to give the faucet a brief turn-on before we let them out, and they drank up the puddles to their hearts' content, then jumped out of the basin and had their romp around the counter. It was easy to guess why Circe had suddenly become so thirsty, since she was providing milk for eight babies. But why had Frisky, too, developed such a passion for water? Finally we noticed that he seemed to have the main job of bathing the babies, by licking them, which must have used up a great deal of moisture. When the litter was weaned, Circe and Frisky quickly lost their need for extra water and ignored the washbasin, only to rediscover it when the next litter was born.

Gerbils will appreciate a sleeping den, although they do not absolutely need one. The simplest way to provide a sleeping den is to place an empty tin can with no sharp edges on its side in the cage. It is amazing how many gerbils can curl up comfortably inside a soup can, all sleeping together.

Sticks, nut shells, and other hard things to chew on are good house furnishings for gerbils, providing work for their busy teeth and discouraging them from chewing on the cage.

For animals as bright and inquisitive as gerbils, another must for the cage is lots of toys and interesting things to do. Exercise wheels and ladders made from wire mesh will provide hours of exercise. The cardboard cylinders that come inside rolls of paper towels and toilet tissue make tunnels that will fascinate gerbils, perhaps because they make the cage more like the burrows of their natural home in the desert. The gerbils seem to enjoy scurrying through the cardboard tunnels and also hopping up on top of them. But they can't seem to resist chewing on the edges of the cardboard and soon reduce the tunnels to scraps of litter. (Fortunately the average family has a steady supply of replacements.)

A few words of caution about where to keep a gerbil cage. Gerbils can tolerate a wider range of temperatures

Exercise wheels . . .

cardboard tunnels . . .

than many animals, so the chances are that anywhere you are comfortable, your gerbil will be too. But never keep a glass or plastic cage in direct sunlight—the "greenhouse effect" can heat up the inside of the cage hotter than even a gerbil can stand. Placing a gerbil cage directly over a radiator is not a good idea either. Nor should gerbils be kept outdoors or in an unheated shed during the cold

and anything else that's handy.

season. (When it gets cold on the Mongolian desert, the gerbils are snug underground in their warm burrows.) If you have a wire cage, you may find your gerbils a bit messy, since they tend to push bedding materials out through the spaces between the wires. Setting the cage on a wide tray or inside a large cardboard box can help to keep the bedding from getting scattered around the room.

One thing to guard against: Don't keep a gerbil cage anywhere that wild rodents might get to it. Mice or rats might be attracted by the odor of the food and gerbil droppings and could spread diseases and parasites. (Wild gerbils normally have their own fleas and other parasites, but these have all been eliminated by gerbil breeders, so the pet gerbils you buy are clean and healthy.)

Another consideration in deciding where to keep a gerbil cage is noise. Gerbils don't seem to mind a normal amount of household bustle, but very loud and sudden noises might frighten them, especially if they are raising a litter. (Don't keep the cage next to the TV when you are watching a Western!) Since gerbils are clean animals, you might be tempted to keep the cage in your bedroom. But then you will probably find that the normal gerbil noises bother *you* too much, particularly since gerbils are active during the night as well as in the daytime. Gerbil babies make a high-pitched squeaking noise, like the peeping of tiny birds. They squeak when they are hungry, they squeak when they are being bathed by their parents, they squeak when they are being moved around—for the first few days it seems as though they are squeaking all the time! As they grow older, they squeak less. When a mature gerbil squeaks, it is usually voicing a complaint, like "Quit shoving!" or "No, you can't have a bite of my sunflower seed! Go find your own!" But gerbils make other noises that may be annoying at times: they chew on the wire or plastic of the cage, or on sticks and nut shells, and scratch vigorously at a wall or corner of the cage, often for minutes on end.

So put your gerbils' cage where they will be safe and comfortable and won't bother anyone—but be sure to keep it in a room where people go frequently. That way the gerbils will quickly grow used to you, and you won't miss any of the fun of gerbil watching.

FEEDING

Most gerbils are willing to try nearly any food that is offered to them. But they do not really *need* such a great variety of food. In the wild, Mongolian gerbils are vegetarians, feeding on plant leaves, tubers, or grains, depending on the season. In homes and laboratories, they thrive on prepared feeds for rodents, which come in convenient dry pellets. You will find a number of brands of feed for gerbils or for gerbils and hamsters in any pet store. Dry dog kibbles and puppy biscuits are also excellent food for gerbils. But in selecting a brand of food for your gerbils, you will have to read the labels carefully. Researchers studying gerbil nutrition have found that for an active, healthy life, and especially to breed successfully and raise healthy litters, gerbils need a feed that is high in protein and not too high in fat. Make sure that the gerbil feed you select contains at least 20 to 24 percent protein. The "birdseed-type" gerbil foods will not pass the label test, for they contain only about 12 percent protein. A gerbil may seem to enjoy such a food, but it will become overweight and not be as healthy as it should be.

A convenience of the dry food is that you can give your gerbils their daily food ration once a day and not have to worry about any excess spoiling or getting moldy. As a general rule, about a tablespoon of food per day for an adult gerbil and about half that for a young one should be ample. But you will quickly get an idea of your own gerbils' appetites and can adjust their food ration accordingly. Don't worry if the gerbils suddenly leave part of their food one day, or another day gobble up everything in sight long before feeding time and seem to be frantically looking for more. Like people, gerbils seem to be hungrier sometimes than at other times; just give them a bit more or less food as they seem to require it. Gerbils will nibble on and off during the day as they get hungry and will eat only what they need. Generally they will not overeat—except with one food: sunflower seeds. Gerbils seem to have a passion for sunflower seeds. If half a dozen kinds of food are

A passion for sunflower seeds.

available, the gerbils will pick out the sunflower seeds first and will stuff themselves, eating one seed after another and coming back for more. Sunflower seeds are fine for gerbil treats, but they should never form too large a part of a gerbil's diet. Sunflower seeds are very high in fat content, and a gerbil eating too many of them will quickly grow overweight.

Though gerbils can thrive on a commercial rodent feed, they do appreciate bits of fresh foods as a change of pace—and if you are raising them without water to drink, fresh foods such as lettuce leaves are a must at least two or three days a week. Fresh foods also provide an extra supply of vitamins and minerals. Be sure to remove any fresh foods that the gerbils do not finish in one sitting, for they can spoil quickly. Though gerbils generally will not eat spoiled foods, a bit of rotting vegetable or fruit can become rather smelly and serve as a breeding ground for harmful germs.

Keeping your gerbils supplied with fresh treats need not be expensive, for gerbils enjoy many things that you might otherwise throw away: the tops and tips that you cut off a carrot, potato peels, apple peels and cores, pea pods (the gerbils eat the whole pod except for the tough strings from the hinges), celery tops, cucumber peels, corncobs (they scoop out the tender morsels you missed, then gnaw on the cobs), and peach pits (crack the pit first, so the gerbils can get to the soft meat inside; they have trouble with hard nut shells). Gerbils will also appreciate an occasional treat of peanuts or nuts, as well as grass, dandelions, and other natural foods.

It is fascinating to watch gerbils eat. A gerbil sits up on its haunches like a squirrel to eat, holding the food in its paws like a sandwich and taking bites out of it. If the original chunk of food is too large to hold up easily (for example, a whole dog biscuit), the gerbil props it up, bites at it until a more convenient-sized piece breaks off, and then holds the piece to nibble on. A lettuce leaf is eaten in much the same way that a gerbil tears up paper—working along the edge, the gerbil punches a series of holes until a strip tears off, except that the gerbil then chews up the strip of lettuce and swallows it, instead of dropping it as it does

Notice how the edge of the lettuce leaf has been nibbled.

with the paper. To eat a sunflower seed, a gerbil uses a special technique. It quickly bites along the seed until the shell splits open lengthwise. It drops the shucked-off shell, quickly turns the seed around and holds it like a candy bar, and bites off pieces from one end to the other.

Gerbils use their front paws so nimbly, like tiny hands, that we wondered whether they ever pick up things with their hands, as people and monkeys do. From what we have observed, gerbils generally pick up things in their mouths, as a dog or cat would, and only then adjust them and hold them in their hands. But this is not always the case. We trained a young litter of gerbils to stand up and beg for sunflower seeds as soon as the top of the cage was opened. As soon as one gerbil got the idea, the others quickly copied him. (Sunflower seeds make ideal rewards for teaching gerbils tricks.) They performed very nicely for several days, each taking a seed and scampering away to eat it, then coming back for more. Then one day, while we were holding out a seed for the next gerbil in line, one who already had a seed in his mouth came back toward the outstretched fingers. We could almost see the thoughts going through his mind. He'd love to have another seed, but his mouth was full. If he opened his jaws to take the new seed, the one he already had would fall out of his mouth. Suddenly he reached out his paws, pulled in the seed, gave a quick pat to readjust the one already in his mouth, stuffed in the second seed too, and scampered away with his booty.

Three other gerbils who observed the new trick stayed for seconds on that round, too.

There is something about a piece of food being eaten by one gerbil that seems irresistible to other gerbils. If you put several pieces of lettuce in a cage with a litter of gerbils, they will all line up along one piece, yanking it back and forth, until it gets so small that some of the gerbils fall off and belatedly discover the other lettuce leaves. When a gerbil is nibbling on a food pellet or a sunflower seed, another one usually comes up and tries to steal a bite. The attempt is met with an annoyed squeak, a little leap, turning around in midair, and the gerbil with the food lands

A piece of lettuce can produce a tug-of-war.

with its back to the moocher. In fact, a gerbil's favorite eating position seems to be facing into a corner. After we hand out sunflower seeds, generally every corner of the cage is occupied by a gerbil, busily munching away, with its back turned to all intruders.

Gerbils' food requirements are so simple and easy to satisfy that family vacations do not usually cause any problems. You may decide to take your pet gerbils along with you. Friends of ours recently took their gerbils on a summer camping trip and said they seemed to enjoy the fresh air. (Some gerbils act sick and listless after a very long drive. Gerbil raisers call this problem "shipping fever" and say that the gerbils quickly recover after a day of rest without food and water.) If you decide to leave your pets home, gerbils can safely stay for up to a week without any attention. Make sure that their cage is escape-proof and out of direct sunlight and drafts, and leave them with plenty of dry food and a fresh bottle of water. (Make sure the bottle doesn't leak!) Chunks of raw potato and carrot will provide some variety and act as an emergency water supply. If you will be gone longer than a week, arrange for someone to come in to check up on your gerbils once a week, feed them, and change their bedding every two or three weeks.

GERBIL WATCHING

One of the reasons we prefer a fish tank for keeping

gerbils is that it provides a wide-open view of all the action. Gerbil watching can be a fascinating activity at any hour of the day or night, for gerbils are active round the clock. There always seems to be something interesting going on in Gerbilville: Perhaps two gerbils are up on their hind legs, boxing in a mock fight that suddenly breaks off as they scamper away to do something else. Gerbils are running in and out of tunnels, playing leapfrog, eating, washing themselves or one another, digging frantically in a corner, sniffing the air, standing up to peer out at you through the glass. . . . Even a sleeping gerbil can be interesting. Many small rodents have one characteristic sleeping position— perhaps curled up into a ball with the nose tucked under and the tail wrapped around. But we have observed gerbils sleeping curled up into a ball, sitting up with the head tucked under, stretched out flat on the stomach, stretched out on the side, lying on the back with feet up in the air (like an opossum "playing possum"), draped over another gerbil like a fur stole, or right in the middle of a whole pile of sleeping gerbils. One researcher reported that a gerbil's sleeping posture varies with the temperature: at or above 86°F the gerbil may sleep on its back with its legs in the air; at about 77°F it tends to lie on its side; and below 77°F it sleeps in a sitting position with the head tucked down between the hind legs. But we observed all these variations and more at room temperatures in the high 60s and low 70s.

Fast asleep.

There are *five* sleepy gerbils in that pile!

A friend to whom we had given a pair of gerbils called us up worriedly the next day. "I'm afraid there's something wrong with the gerbils," she said. "Sometimes when we look at the cage they're not doing anything—just sort of sitting around or sleeping." It turned out that there wasn't really anything wrong with the gerbils. It was just that our friend thought that when we said gerbils are active round the clock, we meant that they are active all the time. Actually gerbils, like other small animals, "live faster" than humans do. Their hearts beat faster, they breathe more rapidly, and their movements are so quick it is sometimes hard to follow them with your eyes. But they are so tiny that they can store up only very small reserves of energy. Many times a day they must stop and nibble on some food or take a little nap to restore their energy.

It is fun watching the gerbils scurry about. Young gerbils are especially bouncy, jumping whenever there is the slightest excuse, or sometimes simply because jumping is more fun than walking. Mature gerbils still jump, but they do not do so as often.

When a number of gerbils are caged together (and sometimes just with a pair), you will see frequent fights, as

Gerbils don't seem to mind getting stepped on.

That boxing match won't last long.

two gerbils bounce up and down on their hind legs like two miniature kangaroos, boxing with their forelegs, or tussle on the floor of the cage, snapping at each other and wrestling for jaw holds. The battles look quite ferocious, but the gerbils are easily distracted and may just get up and go off to do something else as though nothing had happened. Actually nothing has, for there has not been any real biting or scratching, and both gerbils are perfectly unharmed. In fact, such tussles most often end in a grooming session, in which one gerbil lies motionless while the other carefully licks it from one end to the other.

Gerbils seem to enjoy grooming each other and do so frequently. Sometimes two gerbils groom each other at the same time, but more often they take turns. Gerbils also clean themselves frequently, washing themselves with

A gerbil washes itself like a housecat.

tongue or moistened forepaws like a cat. A gerbil can bend and stretch to wash every inch of itself, from its nose to the end of its tail. Some parts, such as the hind legs, are a bit hard to reach, and sometimes the gerbil loses its balance and topples over in the middle of a wash.

When two gerbils meet—for example, when one is returned to the cage after an outing, or even after one gerbil has taken a brief walk to another part of the cage—it is an occasion for a grand reunion. The two gerbils touch noses and sniff each other's heads and sometimes down along the body, with special attention to the scent gland on the belly. Often the mutual sniffing develops into a friendly tussle or a grooming session.

When two strange gerbils meet, the encounter begins the same way, with a sniffing of noses and perhaps a bit of

Sniffing is an important part of gerbil meetings.

licking. But suddenly a genuine fight may develop. Recently we had Circe out meandering on the countertop while we fed the other gerbils. One of the males from her first litter seemed to want to come out of his cage, so we took him out and put him down on the counter to see what would happen. (He was nearly three months old at the time

84

and had not met his mother face to face since he was weaned, at about four weeks.) For a few minutes the two gerbils went their own separate ways exploring around the counter. Finally their paths happened to cross, and they met with obvious interest, sniffing and licking each other's faces. Then suddenly, without warning, Circe lunged at her forgotten son and clamped her jaws somewhere on his underparts. It was a rather confused time while we tried to separate the two gerbils; at first they wouldn't come apart! Finally we picked Circe up by the tail and lifted her until she let go of the other gerbil. He hadn't even squeaked during the struggle, and he seemed quite unhurt. But when we had the two gerbils safely back in their own cages, we found a sizable tuft of belly fur lying on the counter.

One gerbil habit that we found upsetting at first is their vigorous scratching on the walls of the cage, as though trying to dig their way out. A gerbil may continue to do this for minutes on end. We would sit there watching the gerbils scratching away (often the sound of one gerbil scratching will provoke others to start in also) and worry about whether our gerbils were unhappy—they seemed to be trying so desperately to get out. Yet if we opened the cage door and let the gerbils out for a romp on the counter, they would explore for a while, but then of their own accord they would hop right back into the cage. Obviously they considered it their home. Once inside, there they would be, scratching again. Finally we realized that gerbils spend so much time digging and scratching simply because this is a natural activity for them. In their desert home, wild gerbils are continually digging—making and enlarging burrows, opening up plugged entrances, and digging for edible roots and tubers. Some gerbil raisers suggest filling the bottom of their cage with sand. It is a bit too difficult to keep clean for practical purposes, but you can give your gerbils some extra fun by letting them have supervised outings in a sandbox.

More fun can be provided by letting gerbils out to explore in a protected place, such as a bathtub or tabletop. Never leave a gerbil alone on a tabletop or other place from which it might fall. Gerbils normally are cautious at edges and carefully estimate the distance before they will jump

A gerbil usually inspects the situation before it jumps down from a height.

down from a height. But there is always the possibility that the gerbil might slip, or might become so wrapped up in its play that it simply forgets the edge is there.

Interesting toys to explore add more fun for gerbils. Doll furniture and toy cars are just gerbil-sized and will be playfully investigated. But remember that a gerbil will try to chew on everything, so don't offer it any toys that might hurt it.

Toys and other household items can be interesting for a gerbil.

Gerbil racing can be fun.

HANDLING AND TRAINING

A gerbil is much easier to tame than most other animals, for a gerbil is naturally so curious and unafraid that it is ready to do more than half the work itself. In getting acquainted with a new gerbil, first open the cage and hold your hand there, very still. The gerbil will scamper over to sniff at your hand, and may even rest its front paws on your fingers or take a playful nibble at your fingernails. Don't make any sudden, jerky movements or loud noises that might frighten the gerbil; just remain still and talk to it in a calm, gentle voice.

When the cage is open, the gerbil may come over and rest its paws on your hand.

You need not worry about the gerbil's hurting you. Those long, wicked-looking claws are used for digging, not fighting, and the gerbil will not scratch you. A gerbil may occasionally give a person a nip with its teeth, especially if you put your fingers right in front of its face while it is hungry, but the bite is rarely hard enough to break the skin. (If you should ever receive a real bite from a gerbil, puncturing the skin, wash it thoroughly, put some antiseptic on it, and check with your doctor about protection from tetanus, as with any animal bite. Fortunately there have not been any reports of gerbils carrying rabies.)

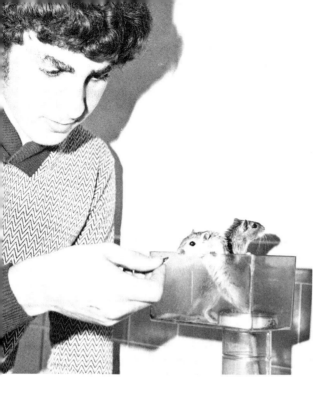

Sunflower seeds are good for taming and training gerbils.

The next step in getting a gerbil accustomed to you is to give it something to eat—preferably a treat it can't resist, such as sunflower seeds or some fresh lettuce or carrot—and scratch it gently on the head or ears while it is eating. Soon you will be able to progress to holding the treats between your fingertips or on your outstretched palm and letting the gerbil pick them up itself. You can also pick the gerbil up and let it explore your hands. The gerbil itself may proceed to this stage, by fearlessly climbing out onto your hand and up your arm. About a week after we had a litter of gerbils trained to beg for sunflower seeds, one of the gerbils suddenly decided that it would be much more interesting to ignore the food and climb out on the hand

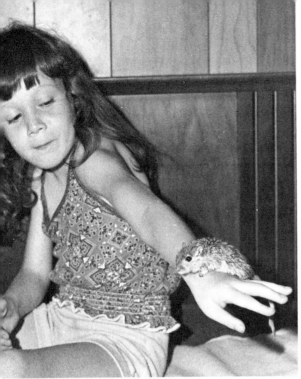 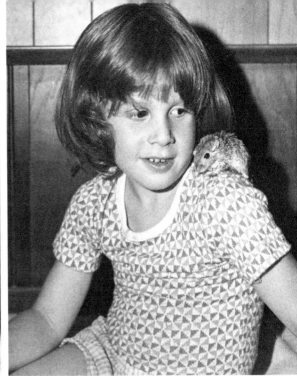

Soon you'll have them climbing your arm . . .

and perching on your shoulder.

instead. We rewarded him by giving him a ride through the air down to the counter, for a fascinating session of exploration. Ever since then, whenever we open the lid of the cage and the other gerbils line up for sunflower seeds, that particular gerbil quickly clambers out for his "magic carpet" ride.

Gradually you can expand your gerbil's repertoire of tricks and allow it more and more freedom. It will enjoy climbing over you and exploring your pockets, especially if you hide an occasional sunflower seed treat inside. Don't

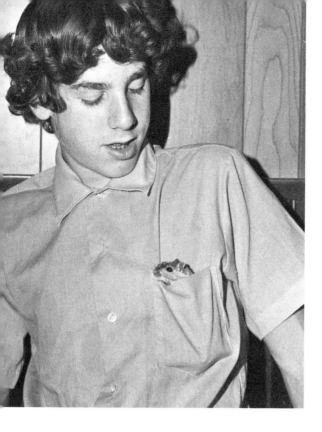

A shirt pocket seems just made for holding a gerbil.

expect a gerbil to sit or lie quietly while you are holding it—its natural curiosity and desire to explore will make it a wriggly passenger.

There are several ways to pick up and hold a gerbil. One is to hold both hands out with the palms turned upward, then bring them together underneath the gerbil, and scoop it up in your cupped hands. Another is to take one hand and close it over and around the gerbil, so that its head sticks out in the opening between your thumb and forefinger and its tail sticks out the other end. (If you pick up a gerbil too rapidly this way, its tail will swing round and round like a pinwheel, as it tries to regain its balance.) Both

You can scoop up a gerbil with two hands . . .   or cup it in one hand.

these methods have some disadvantages: gerbils are so fast-moving and slippery that often you will come up empty-handed—especially since you will not want to squeeze too hard, for fear of hurting the gerbil. Animal breeders usually use a different technique: picking the gerbil up by its tail. This will not hurt the gerbil, if you make sure to grasp the tail near the base, as close to the body as possible. If you grab a gerbil by the end of the tail,

93

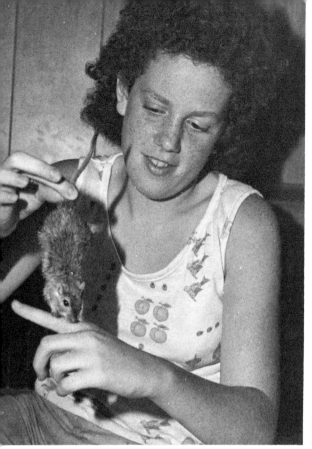 

Gerbil breeders usually pick them up by the base of the tail . . .

but they seem to feel more secure with support for their legs.

the loose skin covering it may tear off, leaving you without the gerbil and the gerbil without the end of its tail! We find that the gerbils seem to feel a bit insecure when they are lifted up by the tail. The best compromise seems to be to grasp the tail with one hand and lift, while quickly slipping the palm of the other hand under the gerbil, so that it will have a firm place to put its feet.

94

Oops!

Handling very young gerbils—up to a month or so—presents special problems. Before their eyes are open, even before they have a full coat of fur, young gerbils are very active. First they wriggle and crawl, and then they begin to scurry and climb and leap. A baby gerbil is so tiny and delicate that you are afraid to squeeze it, yet it can easily wriggle out of your hand if you do not hold it firmly enough. By the time it is a couple of weeks old, it can jump and does so if you try to pick it up. Its eyes may not be open yet, and it doesn't seem to have much sense even if they are. It does not yet know about being cautious of edges and heights and can go hurtling over the edge of a tabletop or squirting out of your hands before you have a chance to react. We haven't lost a young gerbil yet, but we have made a few lucky catches in midair. The moral is: Be sure you are in a secure place when you take young gerbils out to play—a bathtub is just about ideal.

Sometimes when you feel like playing with your gerbils, they may be sleeping. Don't suddenly reach in and grab a sleeping gerbil. If you do, you may upset it—although the gerbils we have known generally wake up much better-tempered than hamsters, which may give you a nasty bite if you disturb their nap. Generally, if you open up the cage and bustle about a bit, perhaps dropping in a small pile of food, the sleeping gerbil will quickly wake up and scamper over to see what is going on. It is amazing what gerbils are capable of sleeping through. We have seen gerbils peacefully snoozing while another gerbil climbs all over them or stands up and scratches noisily on the wall of the cage right next to them. Apparently the gerbil's brain has such noises and disturbances classified as normal events, not worth being bothered about. But let it hear the cage door clink open, or the gentle rustle of other gerbils munching on a fresh lettuce leaf, and the sleeping gerbil is instantly awake. A yawn and a stretch, and it is ready to join the fun. Don't wake your gerbils up too often, though. They need a lot of sleep, and if they miss too much they may be a bit cranky, like a small child who has missed a nap.

One problem that is bound to come up sooner or later when you are handling and playing with gerbils is what to do if the gerbil escapes. Fortunately this is not as much of a problem with gerbils as it is with some other small rodents. A rat or mouse that finds itself free on the floor will head immediately for the darkest corner, under the furniture or into a crack in the wall. If a gerbil falls off a tabletop and lands on the floor, as soon as it has gotten back its wind it will think not about escaping but about exploring. It meanders about, sniffing curiously at everything. Usually you can walk right up to it and pick it up. If it does wander under the furniture or into some other hard-to-get-at place, you can coax it out with a trail of sunflower seeds. A good trick for recapturing a strayed gerbil is to place a cardboard roll from paper towels on the floor, with a few sunflower seeds inside. Don't make a commotion, just wait quietly, and soon the gerbil will be out to explore the enticing tunnel and sample the seeds. As soon as it is inside, you can clap one hand onto each end of the roll, capturing the gerbil. An empty can turned on its side, with some sunflower seeds in it, will work the same trick. Turn it right side up as soon as the gerbil walks into it. Placing the gerbil's cage on the floor near where it escaped can also lure it back. (Remember, the gerbil does not consider the cage a cage—to it the cage is home.)

BREEDING GERBILS

With many pet animals, breeding is a tricky and complicated business. The timing must be perfect: the female must be in just the right part of her reproductive cycle when she and the male are brought together. Otherwise, not only will there be no pregnancy but they may even fight viciously. And, with many animals, the male should never be left with the female while she is raising the young; he may upset her, and he or she may even kill the young. With gerbils there are no such problems, and breeding is a much simpler matter. Once two gerbils have mated, they are happiest together. They arrange their mating at their own convenience, and there is no need to remove the male while the female is raising young. In fact, the father gerbil does his share to help out in child care, washing the babies and retrieving them when they stray.

From the books we read, it all sounded so simple, and everybody we talked to seemed to have more gerbil litters than they knew what to do with. Even our editor told us about a gerbil who was so good-tempered that she gave birth to a litter in the middle of the busy publisher's office and raised it successfully. So why was it that when we were eager to observe gerbils raising their young, we had so much trouble getting started?

Our first experience with gerbils was back in the early 1960s, when they first began to be kept as pets. We got a

98

Both mother and father gerbil share in raising the young.

pair and were impressed with the zeal with which they shredded up a wad of newspaper. (We had to banish them to the hall, because they were at it all night and kept us awake.) But we didn't have that pair of gerbils long enough for them to have young, because we were only keeping them until they were to be used in an experiment at the college. In the years that followed, a number of animals of various kinds moved in and out of our lives, but since gerbils were still rather expensive we did not happen to have any until just before we moved to the country several years ago. No litters from that pair either—they were both males!

By the time we decided to write a book about gerbils, we still had not had the experience of raising gerbil young, and we were very eager to get a pair that would quickly begin producing litters. The most convenient pet shop in our area had such a variety of small animals that they devoted only one display cage to gerbils and generally had only one pair at a time. Their supplier delivered only once a week, which meant that if someone bought the gerbils on display the shop would be out of them until the next shipment. For several straight visits we kept just missing out, arriving at the pet shop the day after someone had bought their only gerbils. Finally we were able to buy a pair of nearly full-grown gerbils, just about the right age for breeding. We watched and waited, but soon it became evident that poor Koko, the female, was not in good health (we'll tell her story later in the chapter), and it began to look less and less likely that she would produce any young.

We began actively to look for some more gerbils. One pet shop was out of them, and our local shop at the time was stuck with the pregnant and nursing pair which couldn't be sold. (We eventually missed out on that pair by just an hour.) In the end we found another shop that did have gerbils in stock, but these were rather young ones, a litter only four weeks old. We picked out a male and a female who were so tiny and cute that we promptly fell in love with them, and settled down to wait. We figured that, with luck, in a little more than a month they might begin to breed. (Gerbils are sexually mature at ten to twelve weeks.) But as the weeks went by, we began to worry. Sweetsie, the female, was so small in comparison with her brother Frisky that we were afraid that she had been the runt of the litter. She seemed active and healthy; in fact, she dashed over more eagerly than Frisky when we opened the cage door and would fearlessly climb up on our hands for an outing. She was a rather scrappy little animal; she usually started the frequent wrestling matches with her brother, and more than held her own. But what if her development had been delayed—or what if she were unable to bear young? We also began to worry about inbreeding: Would there be as good a chance of having healthy young if we mated brother and sister?

About this time our daughter Sharon mentioned that one of her classmates at school had gerbils who had recently had a litter. It turned out that he also had an older litter, almost exactly the same age as our young gerbils. Sharon's classmate was delighted to find a home for two of his gerbils, and when Sweetsie and Frisky were eight weeks old they were introduced to their new mates, Blimpo and

Circe. It was love at first sight. There was not a bit of fighting when the gerbils met. (As a precaution we had been careful to introduce Circe into Frisky's cage and bring Sweetsie and Blimpo together in a new cage, since with many animals the female tends to defend her nest and regards even a prospective mate as a threatening intruder.) In fact, the newly assorted pairs got along together much more calmly than Sweetsie and her brother ever had.

We watched and waited eagerly, and one afternoon, when the gerbils were about ten weeks old, we saw Frisky chasing Circe around the cage. Round and round they went, thumping and clattering, until suddenly Circe stopped, and Frisky briefly mounted her. They separated,

Mating includes many wild chases.

rested for a few minutes, and then started in again, chasing round and round the cage. They went on like that for hours, stopping at times for a bath or a bite of food. Sometimes they stomped their feet at each other (especially Frisky), and sometimes Circe broke away and ran up to the upper compartment to be alone for a while. Sometimes they snatched a brief nap. But then they would be at it again, dashing madly about and pausing briefly to mate. We gleefully jotted a notation down on the calendar, then counted twenty-five days and noted "Circe due." Six days later Sweetsie too had her turn for the courtship chase, and her due date was noted on the calendar.

Days went by and grew into weeks, as we kept waiting.

Sometimes the female stops and lets the male catch her.

Neither of the female gerbils seemed to be getting fat. Perhaps they were going to have small litters. Then, two weeks after Sweetsie and Blimpo had mated—they did it again! Meanwhile, Circe and Frisky had fluffed up their bedding so that it entirely covered the front and sides of the cage, providing them with complete privacy. We didn't know *what* they were doing! Perhaps they were building a nest. But Circe's due date came and went, and no babies arrived. She wasn't even fat—at least not any fatter than usual. (For a long time after we got them, both Circe and Blimpo were somewhat overweight, with especially long, rather shaggy fur, giving them a quite different appearance from the sleek slimness of Sweetsie and Frisky. Apparently Circe and Blimpo's former owner had fed them too much birdseed, and had kept them in a rather cool basement.) Then we began to wonder—it did seem that Circe was getting a bit more pear-shaped than usual. By two weeks after we had originally expected her to give birth it was unmistakable. And two days after that, we happened to walk into the room just in time to watch the birth of her first litter.

Each infant gerbil seemed to come into the world rather easily. Just a grunt and a push and a wriggle, and it slipped smoothly out of its mother's body, wrapped in a membrane like a shiny plastic bag. Circe seemed to know exactly what to do, neatly snipping open the membrane with her teeth and stripping it off, then washing the baby down with her tongue. After each baby, the placenta or afterbirth came out, and although gerbils are normally vegetarians, Circe instinctively ate each one. Eating the placentas gives a number of benefits to an animal mother. The rich nourishment helps to build back the strength she has spent in the labor of giving birth, and the placentas contain hormones that help to stop bleeding and bring her uterus, which has been stretched by the growing babies inside it, back to its normal size quickly.

Circe had a total of eight pups. Each one was about an inch long and weighed about a tenth of an ounce—the weight of a penny. Altogether they added up to a rather sizable fraction of Circe's weight, for she herself weighed only two-and-a-half ounces after the litter was born. (An adult gerbil weighs about two to three ounces, with some older males weighing up to four ounces.)

A newborn gerbil does not look much like its parents. It has a short, stubby muzzle, and it is covered all over with naked, hairless pink skin. Its eyes and ears are sealed tight shut, and its tail is only about a quarter of the length of its body. It looks completely helpless, but it can wriggle and creep a bit, and there is one thing it can do very well: right after it is born, an infant gerbil knows how to nuzzle up to its mother's belly, find a teat amid her fur, and drink the milk that her body produces.

While Circe was having her litter, Frisky became very upset. He dashed back and forth, up and down, trampling the bedding and kicking the pups right and left. After about the fourth birth, he suddenly decided that perhaps Circe wanted to mate and began chasing her and trying to mount her. He soon realized she was not interested, but continued to fuss and fidget, while we watched and worried and wondered what we could do to save the poor mistreated babies. Late that evening, Circe became receptive, and the mating dashes began in earnest. Round and round they went, trampling on baby gerbils and kicking them about like soccer balls. We were convinced that none of the babies would survive. But apparently infant gerbils are not as delicate as they look.

The pups continued to squeak and nuzzle, and each day they grew bigger and stronger. After two or three days, the skin on the pups' backs began to turn dark as the fur began to form. At five days, their ears opened. By seven days, they were covered with a full coat of fine, short fur, dark on the back and light underneath. At ten days, we noticed two dark spots underneath the hindquarters of some of the pups, while others had only a single, much smaller dark spot in the middle. It was easy to tell the sexes of the babies in this way, for the dark spots in pairs were the beginning of the dark pigment that eventually colors the scrotal pouches of the males. At twelve days, the baby gerbils' front teeth appeared. The pups were getting much more active now, constantly crawling away from the pile and being retrieved by their mother or father. (Frisky had quickly calmed down

See how the little gerbils grow.

and begun to enjoy fatherhood, spending many hours a day washing and tending the little ones.)

By about two weeks, the little gerbils were beginning to climb up into the tunnels that connected the cage compartments and were starting to jump, even though their eyes were still tightly shut. Watching them, we wondered how baby gerbils can possibly survive in the wild. We imagined them wandering away from the family nest, getting lost in the mazelike tunnels, and even blundering outside, where snakes and hawks might snap them up. Perhaps they are able to find their way back (or be found by their parents) by smell, and perhaps the plugged entrances help to keep them from wandering out of the burrow. Their tendency to startle and jump at the least provocation may help to protect them from predators until they learn more caution.

All the gerbils we have raised have not opened their eyes until they were twenty or twenty-one days old. But some

Some gerbils open their eyes at 16 days, others much later.

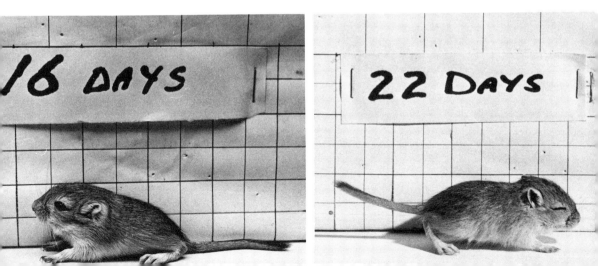

Nursing her babies doesn't keep a mother gerbil from being interested in sunflower seeds.

gerbils open their eyes earlier, as early as sixteen days. (We do not know whether this is a hereditary trait or not; it might be an interesting point to investigate with a breeding experiment.) By the time gerbils are three weeks old, they have begun nibbling on bits of solid food. They can be weaned at any time from three weeks on. If they are left with their mother, she will continue to suckle them for up to six weeks. But it is better to remove them, so that their mother can build up her strength for the next litter, which she may already be carrying.

Circe and Frisky mated the day after the birth of their first litter, and we did not observe them mating at any time after that. When we separated the young gerbils into another cage, at four weeks, Circe was still slim, even though she had already passed the normal twenty-four- or twenty-five-day gestation period. But after another week she began to grow pear-shaped again. Forty-two days after the birth of her first litter, she gave birth to another litter, this time of seven. Apparently while she nursed her large first litter, the new embryos waited inside her body and did not complete their development until after the first litter had been weaned. This time Circe and Frisky were much calmer, more experienced parents and cared for their new babies immediately, with much less fuss and bustle.

We have read that gerbils tend to have about equal numbers of male and female young. That certainly could not be proved by Circe's first litter, which included six males and only two females. In her second litter, the ratio was almost exactly reversed: five females and two males, neatly evening things out. Her third litter had four females and three males. All this proves, of course, is that statistics tend to work best on very large samples—not seven or eight, or even a hundred, but thousands. If all the males and females in a large number of gerbil litters are counted, it turns out that the numbers of each are about equal. But in any single litter, anything can happen—*all* of them may even be of the same sex.

When you have a pair of gerbils and are hoping for a litter, there is not too much you can do to help things out. About a third of all female gerbils have their first litter by three to four months, and most have borne a litter by six months. But there are exceptions: Sweetsie, for example, finally gave birth to a litter of four when she was nine months old, and Koko never produced any young. The female may become pregnant again as soon as her babies are born, and she can continue to bear young until fourteen to twenty months, producing an average of six to seven litters. The size of the litters ranges from one to a dozen, with an average of a little more than four. If you observe the gerbils mating, you may be able to figure out almost exactly when to expect the babies (twenty-four to twenty-

A medium-sized gerbil litter.

five days later). Or you may not have a hint of the coming event until you hear squeaking from the nest. The birth of the litter usually takes only about an hour, and there is nothing you can—or should—do to help the mother. She knows instinctively exactly what to do, and although she will improve with experience, she generally manages well enough even with her first litter. The only contribution you need make is to avoid disturbing her or her babies for about a week. (This is *not* a good time to clean out the cage!) Gerbil mothers are not as excitable as mice or hamsters, and handling very young pups does not cause the mother to kill and eat her young as hamsters do. (She will usually give them a thorough bath, though, as soon as you put them back.) But too much upset during the important first week after birth might cause the mother to trample, smother, or desert her young.

Give the nursing mother extra fluids. A bit of dry milk powder or some small chunks of whole wheat bread soaked in milk are extra treats that can help nourish her as she produces milk for her babies.

Weanling gerbils of several litters can be placed together if you have a large enough cage, as long as they are introduced to each other by a month of age or so. If you leave both sexes together, the gerbils may begin to pair off as they reach sexual maturity. But, to get healthy stock, it is best to avoid too close inbreeding, which means keeping the males and females separated after about eight weeks. In

Junior won't hold still for his bath!

arranging gerbil pairings, a good rule to follow is to mate animals no more closely related than second cousins.

For happy and fruitful gerbil matings, it is best to introduce the prospective couple to each other at about eight or nine weeks, before they have reached sexual maturity. If the gerbils are able to grow into maturity together in this way, there are very rarely any problems with their accepting each other. But older gerbils are rather choosy about their mates. Introductions must be made more cautiously, and it is best to keep them in adjoining cages or compartments with a screen between them for a few days, so that they can get used to each other. Even with these precautions, the gerbils you have planned to mate may not agree with your choice. Sometimes an adult female takes a violent dislike to a male. When they are

113

placed together, she may attack him viciously and even kill him. Or she may accept him as a cage partner but not permit him to mate with her. (In the wild, it is the female gerbil who chooses a mate from the eligible bachelors in the neighborhood.) Fortunately, gerbil breeders have found that such problems do not happen too often—only in about 3 to 5 percent of cases when mature gerbils are mated. So the chances are you will be successful in arranging gerbil matings, even if you are not foresighted enough to bring the animals together while they are young.

YOUR GERBIL'S HEALTH

Gerbils are basically healthy animals and give very few problems to the pet owner. A good diet, sufficient space and ventilation, protection from dampness, drafts, and overheating, and reasonably clean conditions can do a great deal to prevent illness.

Gerbils do not seem to be as prone to diarrhea as some small animals. But if watery stools do develop, cut out fresh greens for several days, change the bedding, and isolate the sick animal. It usually will recover within a few days. (The most common causes of diarrhea are too much roughage in the diet or an infection such as *Salmonella*.)

Gerbils can catch colds, although this does not usually happen. Just as in people, the symptoms are a runny nose, listlessness, and a loss of appetite. Isolate the sick animal and protect it from cold, drafts, and dampness. Vitamin drops, given with a dropper or placed on a piece of solid food, may help.

Sores and minor cuts can be treated with a mild antiseptic. Don't try to apply a bandage. The gerbil will just scratch it off, and may make its injury worse.

Older gerbils often develop a kink or bend in the tail, apparently due to an injury. This does not seem to bother or inconvenience them.

Eye injuries or infections can be treated by bathing the eye with warm water or a solution of Argyrol, or by applying an antibiotic eye ointment.

Bald spots may result from biting by other gerbils, especially if the cage is overcrowded. Or they may be a sign of parasites, such as fleas, lice, or mites. If your gerbils seem to be scratching unusually often or biting at their fur, you

115

may have to apply a flea powder or spray. Use a brand that is safe for cats or hamsters, for, like these animals, gerbils lick themselves and will take in a certain amount of any medication you apply on their fur.

It is fortunate that gerbils so rarely have health problems, for treating a sick gerbil can be a long and discouraging business. We once made the mistake of buying a gerbil whose muzzle was completely bare. Actually she looked rather cute that way, like a miniature koala bear, and we named her Koko. We thought there was probably something lacking in the diet she had been eating at the pet shop. Sure enough, within a week or two of our bringing her home and feeding her plenty of nutritious gerbil food, she sprouted a full new crop of fur on her face and looked like a normal gerbil. We proudly congratulated ourselves on our good management. But unfortunately, a week later Koko's nose was bald again. In the months that followed, she continued to grow new fur and then lose it every few weeks. Observing her more closely, we noticed that she seemed to wash her face much more often than the other gerbils did, and often she seemed to be not only rubbing her face with her paws but actually scratching. Obviously that was how she was losing her hair.

Then Koko developed an infection in one eye. Her continual scratching only made things worse, so that we were afraid she would lose the sight of that eye. Meanwhile, of course, we were trying every remedy we could

Koko kept scratching her nose and irritated her eye.

think of, from vitamin supplements to antiseptics and eye drops. Nothing seemed to help, and Koko became listless and lost weight. Whatever it was that was wrong with her didn't seem to be catching. Her mate Skippy lived in the same cage with her for months, sleeping with her, washing her, and even cleaning her infected eye, but his muzzle remained furry and his eyes bright and clear. Finally Koko did recover from the worst of her illness, although her left eyelids remained permanently a bit swollen and she stayed rather thin even though she had an excellent appetite. But she continued to grow and lose the fur on her muzzle over

117

and over again, and she never mated or bore young even though she and Skippy seemed to have the most tender feelings for each other.

One common gerbil ailment can be frightening to gerbil owners, although it does not seem to bother the gerbils much. Some gerbils develop sudden epilepsylike seizures whenever they are frightened or placed in unfamiliar surroundings. During such a seizure, the gerbil may go into a state like a hypnotic trance, remaining very still with its eyes staring off into space. Or it may go utterly limp, like a rag doll, and appear to be dead. In more severe seizures, the gerbil may twitch spasmodically, or make running motions with its legs, or fall over onto its side. Seizures can be triggered in a susceptible gerbil by such simple things as cleaning the cage or placing the gerbil on an unfamiliar tabletop, or by a meeting with an unfamiliar gerbil—things that would be met with interest by a normal gerbil. Frightening as it may seem, the seizure passes after a few minutes. While it is recovering, the gerbil may seem dazed and groggy, but it recovers completely and acts perfectly normal as long as it is in safe, familiar surroundings.

Both Circe and her brother Blimpo have this epileptic-like trait, but it has not prevented them from living a normal life. Circe has raised large, healthy litters. Of the eight young in her first litter, we have found that one female inherited a very strong tendency to have seizures, while the other female and two of the males sometimes

The excitement of being taken out of the cage and photographed sent Circe into a trancelike seizure.

develop them in situations of great stress. The others in the first litter and all seven of the second seem to be normal, just like their father, Frisky. Researchers are not sure why seizures are so common among gerbils (much more common than in other laboratory animals such as rats and mice) and what causes them. Seizure-prone gerbils are being actively studied, since it is hoped that such study will help in understanding epilepsy in humans and in developing treatments and cures.

If one of your gerbils has a seizure, don't panic. (No deaths from this condition have ever been observed.) Don't try to push it or prod it or shake it; that would only frighten it even more and delay its recovery. Just pick it up gently and place it back in its own familiar cage. The other gerbils will come over to sniff at it, apparently wondering why it does not get up and play. But in a few minutes it will gradually recover and soon be running around like its old self again.

GERBILS AND OTHER PETS

If you have some other family pets, you may be wondering how gerbils would get along with them. It is sometimes possible to keep gerbils with other small rodents, if they are raised together from a very early age. (This does not go for hamsters, which are so aggressive that they should not be caged with anything—not even another hamster.)

With larger pets, it is usually necessary to be sure the gerbils are securely caged, for their own protection. A dog or cat may not realize that a pet gerbil is special—it looks too much like a mouse or rat. Perhaps you have seen pictures of cats or dogs living peacefully with mice or other rodents. Some adult cats or dogs can be taught to accept rodents, but the trick usually is to introduce them when the cat or dog is very young and has not yet learned to hunt. A friend of ours had a gerbil and a mouse, who lived together in a rather broken-down cage with a door that wouldn't stay shut. This meant that both the gerbil and the mouse had the run of the whole house, but they always came back to their cage to sleep. The family had a house cat who was familiar with the rodents and never bothered them. But they had another cat who lived out in the barn. One day he slipped into the house, and that was the end of the gerbil.

Our cats are fascinated by our gerbils and sneak into the room where they are kept every chance they get. (We usually keep the door closed, fearing that the cats may knock down one of the cages.) One day we tried introducing our latest kitten, Muffin, to the gerbils. Muffin was only about five weeks old at the time, and she had not yet had any lessons in mouse catching. We opened the cage and watched. Muffin was entranced. She didn't make any attempt to catch the gerbils, though she carefully watched every move they made. The gerbils seemed quite unconcerned and unafraid. They popped in and out of their cage and scampered about right alongside the kitten. Once

Muffin was fascinated by the gerbils.

Muffin reached a paw into the cage and patted one of the gerbils. It wasn't the kind of tap a full-grown cat will give a mouse that it is playing with; it was a gentle, stroking pat down the gerbil's back, very much like the pats Muffin herself receives from us.

Another time we decided to see how Muffin's mother, Kally, would react to gerbils. Kally is an experienced mouser. We had recently transferred a litter of month-old gerbils to a large aquarium, furnished with wood shavings and an assortment of cardboard tubes for tunnels and two empty cans for nesting boxes. Normally the aquarium is a madhouse, with gerbils everywhere, scampering into the tubes and popping out, leaping, boxing, and standing up to look around like tiny prairie dogs. We carefully lowered Kally into the enclosure, standing by ready to swoop down and grab her if necessary. The little gerbils had never seen a cat before, but they seemed to sense that something was going on. They all disappeared instantly, popping into the closest tube or can. Kally bent down and peered into the nearest open end. Immediately, behind her back, a gerbil head popped out of the other end of the tube and looked at her. She heard the movement and turned her head. The gerbil disappeared into the tube, and at the same instant heads popped out of the other end and out of the two cans. The cat looked back, the heads retreated, and the other one popped out again. Back and forth the game went on for a few minutes, until Kally grew bored and tried to stir up a bit more action by tapping the tubes. When that got no results and she decided to dig some gerbils out of a can with her paw, we broke up the sport and took her out. As soon as the cat was gone, the gerbils were all out running around their cage again.

WHAT NOT TO DO WITH EXTRA GERBILS

When you have a contented pair of gerbils and let nature take its course, it is easy to wind up with more gerbils than you intended. A single female, having just an average number of average-sized litters, can produce more than two dozen offspring during the year or so she is actively reproducing. And each of her young is itself capable of fathering or bearing an equal number more.

Sometimes pet shops are glad to take excess gerbils, as long as they are clean and healthy. School friends are also good prospects. An ad in a local paper may bring results. If you intend to sell your gerbils or give them away, be sure to keep careful records, so that you know exactly how old each gerbil is, whether it has mated, and how many young, if any, it has borne.

If you are having trouble giving away some extra gerbils, you may be tempted to just take them out into a field or vacant lot and let them go. It may seem kind to let them enjoy their freedom. But in the long run, releasing animal pets in this way is neither a kind nor a wise thing to do. The most likely fate for a gerbil set free in a field or lot is to be gobbled up by a prowling cat. Tame gerbils have never known what it is like to have to live by their wits; they have never known danger. They are so unafraid that they may walk right up to a cat or dog and sit there looking at it. If released gerbils do manage to survive the attacks of predators and dig a system of burrows as wild gerbils do in their native home, flooding rains or winter cold may wipe them out. If they survive all these hazards and become firmly established in an area, the results may eventually be even worse.

Every wildlife community exists in a delicate balance. Some animals feed on the plants, and are in turn preyed on by other animals. Each helps to keep the others in balance.

Gerbils released in a field could become pests.

If the predators were killed, for example, the prey animals would multiply. But then they might eat too much of the plant life and ultimately starve. When a new species is introduced into a balanced natural community, no one can predict for sure what changes will occur. Picture a meadow, for example, in which rabbits and field mice scurry among the grasses, and snakes, owls, and foxes prey on them and help to keep them from multiplying. Now add a colony of gerbils. The foxes, snakes, and owls will probably add gerbils to their diet. But gerbils, mice, and rabbits can reproduce faster than the predators can. Perhaps the predators, catching gerbils now, will not be as hungry and will not catch as many mice and rabbits. The rabbits may have a population explosion and eat the grass of the meadow right down to the roots, so that the land becomes barren. Or the mice might multiply and invade nearby farmers' fields. Eventually the foxes and owls and snakes will catch up and bring the meadow community back into balance. But it will be a different balance than before. And all the changes will have occurred because some kindhearted person dropped off a few extra pets to enjoy a taste of freedom.

Gerbils in the Laboratory

Victor Schwentker's hope, in bringing Mongolian gerbils to the United States, was to introduce a valuable new research animal. Researchers responded with enthusiasm. Here was an unusual opportunity: a brand-new research animal, about which very little was known, which now could be bred and studied in the laboratory in unlimited numbers.

It is not often that a new animal suitable for laboratory studies is discovered. Some animals have very specialized food requirements which cannot easily be satisfied in the laboratory. (The koalas of Australia, for example, eat only eucalyptus leaves.) Some animals are naturally so timid and excitable that they cannot be tamed and never settle down enough to breed in the laboratory. Some animals, in fact, are so upset at being captured that they cannot survive in captivity—they promptly go into shock and die. So researchers happily seized the new opportunity and plunged into studies of gerbils—their behavior, their growth and

The breeder room at Tumblebrook Farm.

development, their needs in food, housing, and care, their heredity, and the diseases to which they are susceptible.

These studies led to new ideas on how gerbils could be used to expand our knowledge of the living world and help to control some of the diseases and other problems that plague mankind. In the relatively short time since gerbils were introduced, many hundreds of reports have been published in scientific journals, describing the use of gerbils in experiments in such fields as aerospace, aging, bacterial and viral diseases, behavior, cancer, dentistry, drug research, ecology, endocrinology (the study of hormones), genetics, heart disease, metabolism (the chemical reactions in the body), neurology, parasitic diseases, psychology, and radiation. Gerbil studies helped in the development of live polio vaccines and birth control pills and are helping medical researchers gain insights into the role of cholesterol and fats in heart disease. These little animals have already helped to save countless numbers of human lives.

BEHAVIOR AND PSYCHOLOGY

Many of the early studies of gerbil behavior reported the same kind of fascinating details of daily life that an observant pet owner can note for himself: courtship and mating practices, grooming sessions, and sleeping positions, for example. Delbert Thiessen's group at the University of Texas at Austin has gone much deeper into gerbil behavior, with a series of studies focusing on gerbils' scent glands and their defense of their home territory.

Adult gerbils, both males and females, have a special gland on the underbelly, which produces an oily substance (sebum) with a distinctive odor. Researchers noticed that the gerbils frequently mark objects in their environment—

The fur on this gerbil's belly has been cut away to show the scent gland.

sticks, stones, even other gerbils. Males have a larger scent gland than females and do more scent marking. One series of experiments established that scent marking is linked with the sex hormones. If a male gerbil's testes are removed, his scent gland shrinks and his marking behavior decreases rapidly. Injections of testosterone (a male sex hormone) reversed the effect, and with large amounts of the hormone the males became "supermarkers," marking about three times as often as usual. A special part of the brain controlling the scent marking behavior was also discovered.

After exploring the "how" of scent marking, the researchers progressed to the "why": Just what does scent marking mean to gerbils, and what role does it play in their

The gerbil is scent marking a peg in an activity box.

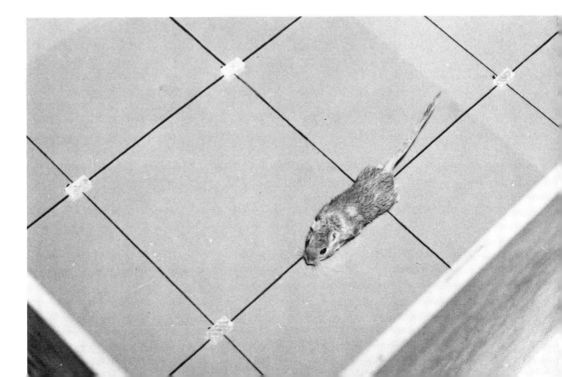

life? Many animals use odor-producing chemicals to communicate with others of their kind, laying odor trails or setting down chemical "no trespassing signs" at the boundaries of their territories. Ants, for example, use odors to lead others of their nest to food and to signal relationships among the queen, workers, soldiers, and young in the anthill. Ants' behavior is not very flexible; an ant will react to a particular odor or other stimulus in exactly the same way every time, no matter what the circumstances might be. For example, a dead ant gives off an odor that signals to the living ants in the colony that it should be carried out of the anthill and dumped. Researchers sprayed the "dead ant" odor on a live ant. Workers in the anthill promptly picked up the sprayed ant and carried it out, even though it was wriggling and squirming and not acting dead at all.

Studies of gerbil scent marking revealed that their scent does not have such a rigid meaning, and their behavior is much more flexible. When a gerbil is offered two objects, one of which has been marked with gerbil scent, it will invariably investigate the scent-marked object first. But it quickly loses interest, and does not show any preference for either object the next time it is offered the same choice. If, however, a social interaction such as mating or fighting with a strange gerbil occurs between the two tests, the gerbil's interest in the scent secretion remains high. Hungry gerbils also quickly learned to use a mark of scent on rocks as a signal that food pellets were hidden underground in that spot.

Further studies showed that in normal gerbil life the scent marking is associated with territorial behavior. Pairs of gerbils were housed in walled-off areas which could be connected by opening small trapdoors in the walls. Whenever a connecting door was open, the gerbils (especially the males) would begin to fight, each defending his own territory. Acts of scent marking became much more frequent than when the gerbils lived in isolated pairs. Often one gerbil was more aggressive than his neighbor, and the neighbor gave up the fight. The winner claimed the new

The laboratory floor was divided into walled-off "territories."

territory, and his scent marking behavior increased, especially in the new territory, while the loser no longer marked at all.

For some animals, losing a territorial dispute is such a crushing blow that the loser becomes unable to mate and live normally, and he may even pine away and die. The researchers thought that the stress of losing might make gerbils unable to mark again. Instead, they found that when a defeated male was moved to a new, unowned territory, his marking behavior quickly returned to normal. But if the soiled sawdust and droppings from the old territory were moved into the new territory, the loser did not mark, apparently obeying the chemical signals even though his conqueror was no longer present.

Female gerbils have another use for their scent gland. While a female is nursing a litter, her scent gland enlarges, and her marking behavior becomes much more active. The favorite objects of her marking are her own pups, and the scent helps her to find them when they stray. If the sebum from a female gerbil's scent gland is smeared on a pup from another mother, she will retrieve the foster pup just like her own.

In another experiment exploring gerbils' territorial behavior, male and female intruders were introduced one at a time into a territory in which a pair of gerbils was already living. This territory was separated from a safe, unoccupied territory by a water barrier (an aquarium). Normally gerbils prefer not to swim. But the intruders were immediately attacked by the resident pair so viciously that they either were killed or chose to swim away to safety. Later, if the animals who had migrated safely across the water were given a choice of two cages, one that was clean and one that contained some litter and droppings from the territory where they had been defeated, nearly all of them chose to make a nest in the cage with clean shavings. (Gerbils who had never met the victorious defenders and had never had the experience of migrating were equally likely to choose either of the cages.)

In some psychology experiments, gerbils have shown themselves to be rather bright. For example, gerbils can learn an avoidance response about ten times as rapidly as rats. In this kind of experiment, the animal must learn, for example, that when it hears a special sound signal, it must press a lever; otherwise, it will receive some form of punishment, such as an electric shock. Gerbils also do well in tests in which they must choose among an assortment of up to four objects. But in one favorite type of psychology experiment, gerbils look like absolute dunces: they are no good at running mazes. A rat or mouse can learn fairly easily to go through a rather complicated maze, making the correct choice at each turning and avoiding all the blind alleys to reach a food reward at the end. A gerbil finds the maze itself far more interesting than the reward. Even if the gerbil has been starved for a day, and a tempting pile of

This box is designed to test the gerbil's ability to judge depth. An observer is testing to see whether the gerbil will show caution at the edge of an apparent drop.

sunflower seeds is placed at the exit, it will persist in exploring the entire maze, stopping to investigate each dead end, before it finally meanders its way out.

Gerbils' high aptitude in learning avoidance responses led to their being involved in one of the most fascinating and far-out lines of scientific research, and then in a scientific scandal. The field was parapsychology, the study

Gerbils are not very good at running mazes—they are more interested in exploring than in getting to the end.

of abilities of the mind that are beyond what is usually considered normal. Have you ever dreamed of something and then had it actually happen? Have you ever suddenly thought about someone you hadn't seen in years, and then the telephone rang and he or she was calling? Have you ever had someone say exactly what you were thinking, as though he or she were reading your mind? Many people have had experiences that are difficult to explain without assuming that some kind of ESP (extrasensory perception) is operating. Scientists in a number of laboratories are studying people who have experiences such as these. But this is a difficult and frustrating field of study. People who claim to have ESP—to be able to know what other people are thinking or foretell the future—usually cannot control their ability. Under the strict conditions of the laboratory, with scientists staring at them, people tend to "freeze up," and any parapsychological ability they may have disappears. Then, too, many people who claim to have "psychic powers" are really cheating. It has been so difficult to get repeatable results in parapsychological experiments that many scientists do not believe ESP really exists.

To get around these difficulties, researchers at the Institute for Parapsychology at Durham, North Carolina, got the idea of using animals, which would not cheat or "freeze up" in the experiments. Gerbils and hamsters were selected for a series of experiments on precognition, the ability to foretell the future. A simple setup was used. Electric wires were connected to a metal cage. A gerbil was placed in the cage, and then a mild electric shock was delivered to one side of the cage. If the gerbil happened to be on the side of the cage that received the shock, it promptly jumped over to the other side. But sometimes the gerbil was observed to jump over to the safe side *before* the electric current arrived. Either it was just lucky, or somehow it seemed to know in advance which side of the cage would receive the electric shock. The experiments were set up so that the electric shocks were delivered automatically—even the researcher did not know in advance which side of the cage would receive a particular shock.

A variety of results was obtained. Sometimes the animals jumped after the shock hit, and sometimes before. Sometimes they jumped into the correct side, and sometimes they made the wrong choice. But it seemed that a little oftener than not, they were guessing right. Complicated mathematical analyses were used to determine if the small difference was really significant, or if it was just happening by chance. These analyses showed that the difference was real—gerbils and hamsters actually seemed to be able to foretell the future!

Then the scandal broke. In the summer of 1974 it was revealed that the director of the research had cheated on a later experiment; he had adjusted the computer that was controlling the study and analyzing the results so that a significant difference would be obtained. The researcher resigned, explaining that he had yielded to temptation when he was unable to repeat the positive results he had obtained at first. But now no one knew for sure whether any of his previous work had been trustworthy. It was a very sad affair, in which the career of a promising young researcher was ruined and clouds of doubt were again cast on the field of parapsychology, which had at last been achieving a degree of respectability.

A more encouraging story of gerbils and psychology has

been that of their use in helping emotionally disturbed children. Many psychologists believe that owning a pet is a particularly valuable experience for a child. The child receives love and attention from his pet and learns to take responsibility, for his pet is completely dependent on him. If he does not feed and care for it, it may become ill or even die. For emotionally disturbed children, pets can be especially helpful. The child may have difficulty relating to adults or other children, and his inability to communicate or his disruptive behavior may make others dislike him. But with an animal pet he does not have to put up a front. The animal accepts and loves him uncritically, and gradually he learns to give his love in return. A relationship with a pet may act as an opening wedge in teaching the disturbed child to get along better with people and to feel better inside about himself. Dr. Frances Ilg, a noted child psychologist at the Gesell Institute at Yale, has used "gentle gerbils" to help emotionally disturbed children.

DISEASE STUDIES

One of the earliest contributions gerbils made as a laboratory animal was in the study of a disease called bilharziasis. This serious disease is caused by a parasitic worm, which is carried by freshwater snails and multiplies in its victim's body, causing dysentery and loss of blood.

Health officials estimate that bilharziasis afflicts about 200 million people, including three-quarters of the population of Egypt. In 1950 researchers reported on bilharziasis experiments in Egypt, using gerbils that they bought for two piastres each from sellers who obtained the rodents from Bedouin catchers. The gerbils they used were the local species, *Gerbillus gerbillus*.

Since then, with the development of the Mongolian gerbil as a commonly available laboratory animal, the use of gerbils in disease research has widened greatly. Gerbils have been used to study parasitic diseases, such as leptospirosis and tapeworm, and bacterial diseases, such as tuberculosis, anthrax, and leprosy. They are particularly susceptible to viral diseases, especially respiratory viruses and viruses that attack the nervous system, and they played an important role in the development of the oral live polio vaccine.

For a number of years, heart disease researchers have been keenly interested in the role of cholesterol and fats in the gradual narrowing of the arteries that can lead to a heart attack. They find gerbils especially interesting. Gerbils develop unusually high levels of cholesterol in their blood, even on a normal diet with a fat content of only 4 percent. People with high levels of blood serum cholesterol usually develop thick deposits of fatty substances in their arteries, but gerbils do not. Researchers hope that if they can discover the secret of gerbils' resistance to cardiovascular disease, they may find clues to ways of decreasing the terrible toll of heart disease in humans.

Gerbils are also being used in research on cancer. The first published report on the new variety of black gerbils dealt with their use in the study of melanoma, a kind of cancer in which the diseased cells contain a dark-colored pigment.

Gerbils can develop cavities in their teeth and are susceptible to various diseases that affect the structures that support the teeth. Dental researchers are using gerbils in studies of the role of bacteria in tooth decay.

A cancerous tumor developed on the hind leg of one of the first black gerbils. It was successfully removed by surgery.

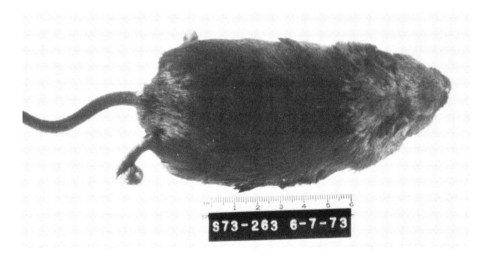

Scientists are studying epilepsylike seizures in gerbils for clues that may help human epileptics. This gerbil's brain waves are being recorded through electrodes implanted in its brain.

One of the most intriguing uses of gerbils in medical research is in the study of epilepsy. The spontaneous seizures that many gerbils have are quite unusual in laboratory animals, and they are very similar to the seizures of humans suffering from epilepsy. Researchers studying seizure-prone gerbils have implanted electrodes in their brains and recorded their brain waves. (This procedure does not hurt or even bother the gerbils.) They have found that seizures in gerbils do not seem to be caused by a vitamin deficiency, or by overcrowding. Seizures can be set off by handling, rapid change of temperature or lighting, and confinement in small areas. (One researcher found he could even produce seizures just by lifting the gerbils' cage

One experimenter used this open field activity box to test all his gerbils for a tendency to have seizures in new surroundings. Then each of the seizure-prone animals was placed in the box every day. After five days, the box had become so familiar that none of them had seizures there. But after a week without seeing the box, some of the gerbils had seizures in it again. The antiepileptic drug Dilantin prevented the seizures.

a few inches above its normal shelf level.) Susceptible gerbils have been found to be more prone to have seizures in the nighttime, when they are most active, than during the day. It was found that the same drugs that are effective in controlling seizures in human epileptics can also prevent seizures in gerbils. Researchers are using gerbils as test animals in the development of new drugs for epileptics, and they are trying to breed lines of gerbils that are especially susceptible to seizures for use in this work.

TISSUE TRANSPLANTS

There are many people alive today who would have died if they had not received a kidney, transplanted from another person. A number of other organs have also been transplanted, some successfully, others not so successfully. For a while, heart transplants were making the news, as surgeons used this dramatic operation in the fight to save lives. But after a year or two, heart transplants became rare. Too many patients were dying after successful operations, because their own bodies' defenses over-whelmed the transplanted heart. Special cells in the body have an amazing ability to recognize the difference be-tween the thousands of chemicals normally found in the body and "foreign" chemicals that may be introduced. This system normally works smoothly in helping the body to fight disease germs, which are recognized as foreign and attacked. But each person has an assortment of body chemicals that is different from everyone else's. One person's heart may look like another's, and work the same way, but it is not exactly the same chemically. The body considers a transplanted heart as foreign and rejects it, so it dies. And then the patient dies too. Drugs can be used to lower the body's defenses and prevent rejection of the transplant; but then the body's defenses against diseases are lowered too, and the person may die of a bacterial infection that he is no longer able to fight.

Researchers are trying to find better ways to combat rejection and make transplants of foreign tissues and organs successful. Gerbils are playing a key role in such studies. For gerbils and hamsters are the only small mammals found so far that can accept a foreign tissue graft, even from randomly bred animals. They do not reject the grafts, and yet they can protect themselves against infection by invading disease germs. If researchers can find out how the gerbils' tolerance to tissue transplants works, they may be able to apply the knowledge to humans and be able to replace diseased organs and tissues more successfully. Such investigations can also help in the study of cancer and endocrine functions.

RADIATION STUDIES

A person may be exposed to quite a bit of radiation in his

lifetime. The radioactive fallout from nuclear explosions has received the most publicity, but there are also cosmic rays from space and radiation from the naturally radioactive minerals of the earth's crust. Even diagnostic X-rays can have an effect on the body, and medical researchers are constantly discovering ways to use radiations to treat cancer and other diseases. Naturally scientists are trying to find out as much as they can about how radiation affects living tissues, and they have found the gerbil a particularly interesting experimental animal. A gerbil can stand about twice as much radiation without harm as a rat or mouse can.

If scientists could find out why the gerbil's natural radioresistance is so high, they might gain some valuable clues to how to protect humans from the damaging effects of radiation. Soviet researchers have found that the saying "You are what you eat" may be truer than we realize. They made a careful study of what a population of wild gerbils was eating, gathered supplies of all the seeds and leaves in the gerbils' natural diet, and fed them to white rats. Then they tested the rats' response to irradiation and found that their radioresistance was much higher than that of rats fed the usual laboratory diet. Now they are trying to find out what factors in the gerbils' diet provide the protection, in hopes of developing some radioprotective drugs that could be used for people.

Experimenting with animals can be both interesting and fun. Gerbils are such gentle, yet lively animals that they are ideal subjects for a number of scientific experiments that you can do yourself.

First of all, you can act as a naturalist and observe the gerbils' behavior. You might want to simulate the gerbils' natural habitat by partly filling a large aquarium with a moistened mixture of one part sand to two parts soil, with rocks and live plants to complete the effect. Keep a notebook and record everything you see the gerbils doing, and how they do it. If you have trouble telling the gerbils apart, you can mark each one with a colored spot on the top of its head, using food coloring or a smear of ink from a felt-tipped pen (the nontoxic kind). After you mark the gerbils, keep them apart until the ink or dye dries, so that they will not lick one another. (In a few days the marking will wear off, as the gerbils wash themselves and one another.)

One problem that naturalists have in observing animals is that the animals react to the presence of the human observer and may not act naturally. What the naturalist sees may not be the way the animals behave when they are not being observed. There are several tricks you can use to keep your gerbils from realizing you are watching them. Scientific supply houses sell one-way aluminized foil, which you can place over the front of their enclosure. (You will be able to see in, but the gerbils will not be able to see out.) Be careful not to make distracting noises while you watch. You can keep your scent from reaching the gerbils by setting up a small fan, blowing from the cage toward you. You can observe gerbils' nighttime behavior by placing them in a darkened room, lighted only by a red light. (Gerbils, like many other animals, have very poor red vision and will think it is dark.)

Vary the experiments by changing the gerbils' environment and seeing how they react and how they use different materials. Do they build the same kind of nest with tissues as they do with grass or hay? Do they try to burrow into a thick layer of wood shavings as they do in sand?

A tape recorder can help make your observations of gerbil activities more meaningful. Switch on the recorder and let it run. Each time you notice gerbils doing something—jumping, playing tag, sniffing or licking each other, eating, curling up to sleep—call out the activity and say which gerbil is doing it. Later, when you replay the tape, use a stopwatch or a watch with a second hand to record how often each type of activity occurred and how long it went on. (You might have a series of sessions, each time focusing on a particular animal or on a particular kind of activity, for example grooming.)

Some animals that live in groups have been found to set up a "pecking order." One dominant animal has a variety of privileges, such as first turn at the feeding dish and the best nesting quarters, and it is invariably victorious in fights with other animals of the group. The other group members are arranged in order with decreasing privileges, until the last, the "born loser" who is picked on by everyone else and is last in line at the feeding dish. Pecking orders have been observed in chickens, mice, goats, and other animals. See if you can determine such a ranking in a group of gerbils living together in a large cage.

Some researchers have reported that male gerbils tend to dominate females, driving even their mates away from the feeding dish until they have eaten their fill. Among the gerbils we have observed, feeding time was usually a free-for-all. The only clear case of dominance was exactly the reverse of the researchers' reports. Skippy (a male) always let his mate Koko eat first when a new supply of food was placed in the cage. When there was an especially tempting tidbit, such as lettuce or sunflower seeds, he would slip in, grab a piece, and dash away to another part of the cage to eat it. Otherwise, he would wait his turn until Koko had satisfied her hunger.

In observing gerbil behavior, you must remember that gerbils, like people, are individuals and may vary from the "usual" behavior for their species. Skippy, for example, was a particularly industrious personality and took complete charge of the housekeeping chores, continually moving and rearranging the bedding and "sweeping" the upper room clean. In other pairs, the female seemed more concerned with such matters, and in still others both sexes shared their duties about equally. Scientists build up a picture of what is the normal behavior for a species by putting together observations of many different animals.

You can determine gerbil activity as scientists do. One way is to hook up an exercise wheel to a tally register, which will register a number each time the gerbil turns the wheel. Or you can make up an activity box, by lining the bottom of a large cardboard box with a sheet of paper, ruled in four-inch squares, numbered in order. Place the gerbil in square 1, then record the sequence of numbers of each square it enters. If you have a rat or mouse or can borrow one from a friend, it will be interesting to place it in

This is one type of apparatus scientists use to study gerbil activity. An automatic counter tallies the number of times the gerbil turns the wheel.

You can make some simple setups out of a cardboard box . . .

the same activity box (alone, not with the gerbil!) and compare its behavior. Researchers have found that a rat or mouse tends to stay closer to the walls of such a box, while gerbils move more fearlessly across the open spaces.

Vary the experiment by gluing a small pebble in the center of each numbered square, and see whether the gerbil uses his scent gland to mark the pebbles. If he does, take him out and place another gerbil of either sex in the box. Does it seem interested in sniffing the scent-marked pebbles?

Psychological studies are always fun. A simple T-maze or

or some blocks.

a more complicated construction will quickly give you an idea of why scientists sometimes feel frustrated. Can you think of something besides sunflower seeds that would give the gerbil more motivation to stick to his job? (Perhaps a cage with his mate at the end of the maze?)

Some physiological experiments will help you get to know more about gerbils and about yourself. Listen to the gerbil's rapid heartbeat with a stethoscope and time it with a watch, then compare it with your own pulse rate. Count the number of breaths a gerbil takes each minute, and then have someone do the same for you. (Your friend should wait

151

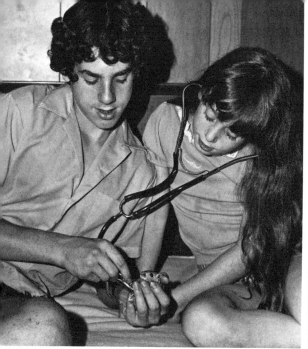

A gerbil's heartbeat is faster than yours.   How fast does the gerbil grow?

to observe you when you aren't thinking about it anymore.) Do the gerbil's heartbeat and respiration rate change after it has been running on an exercise wheel?

Try weighing the amount of food you give your gerbils each day; then weigh the amount that is left over after twenty-four hours. (You may have to go hunting through the litter for half-eaten tidbits to get a more accurate count.) Do gerbils eat the same amount each day? Do they eat the same amount if you feed them different kinds of food each day?

It's fun to study gerbil food preferences. Place two kinds of food in front of the gerbil, in two piles a few inches

152

apart. Note which kind of food it selects. If it shows a preference for one kind over another, then the next day eliminate the less-preferred food and substitute another. Note which food the gerbil prefers this time. Continue comparing foods until you have built up an idea of the gerbil's likes and dislikes. Try this with several gerbils, and see whether they all like the same foods or have individual preferences. You can try the various brands of standard gerbil foods (one type comes in three flavors, and our gerbils all seem to prefer two of them to the other) and also such "people foods" as potato chips, popcorn, and dry cereals, and natural products such as nuts, fruits, seeds, bark, roots, and leaves. Gerbils are normally vegetarians, but see how they react to meat, egg, and insects or mealworms. Most gerbils will at least try a nibble, and some seem to like them very much.

Add to the pleasure of breeding gerbils by doing it scientifically. Keep careful records of the parents of each gerbil and any unusual characteristics it has—fur color, shape of nose or ears or tail, unusual aggressiveness, shyness or adventurousness, a tendency for seizures—and try to determine whether they are hereditary by tracing them down the gerbil family tree. Weigh the young gerbils each day as they grow, and then every week when they are older. Do they gain more weight on a particular brand of food? Does a litter raised with a water bottle after weaning do better than one that receives all its moisture from fresh

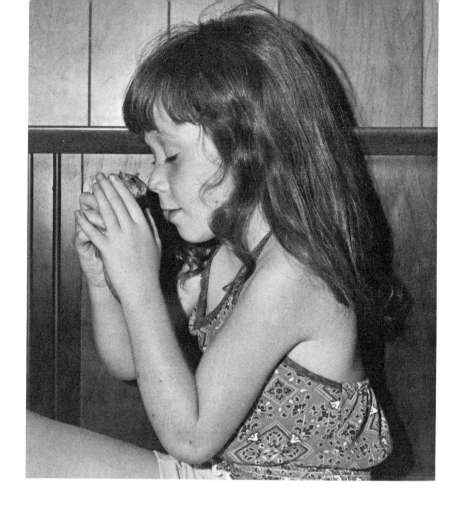

greens? What will happen if you give your gerbils only dry foods for a week or two?

The gerbil was first bred as a laboratory animal, and it has already more than fulfilled all the researchers' hopes. But perhaps this little animal has an even greater contribution to make as a pet. Its lively curiosity, gentle nature, and harmonious family life have endeared the gerbil to millions of children and adults.

For Further Reading

Dobrin, Arnold. *Gerbils*. New York: Lothrop, Lee and Shepard, 1970.

Monroe, Barbara Nippert. *Gerbils in Color*. Neptune, N. J.: T. F. H. Publications, 1970.

Robinson, D. G., Jr. *How to Raise and Train Gerbils*. Neptune, N. J.: T. F. H. Publications, 1967.

———. *Know Your Gerbils*. Harrison, N. J.: Pet Library, 1973.

Schwentker, Victor. *The Gerbil: An Annotated Bibliography*. West Brookfield, Mass.: Tumblebrook Farm, n.d.

Shuttlesworth, Dorothy. *Caring for Gerbils and Other Small Pets*. New York: Scholastic, 1970.

Gerbil Suppliers

Spot mutants are distributed by Haley Farm, Route 2, Box 81, Hurt, Virginia 24563.

Black mutants are distributed by Tumblebrook Farm, West Brookfield, Massachusetts 01585.

Index

77-216

ALVIN SILVERSTEIN, born in New York City and raised in Brooklyn, developed an early interest in science. He received his B.A. from Brooklyn College, his M.S. from the University of Pennsylvania, and his Ph.D. from New York University. He is a professor of biology at the Staten Island Community College of the City University of New York.

VIRGINIA B. SILVERSTEIN grew up in Philadelphia and received her B.A. from the University of Pennsylvania. Since her marriage, she has worked as a free-lance translator of Russian scientific literature, doing extensive work for government and private agencies.

The Silversteins, who have collaborated on more than forty science books for young readers, live on a farm near Lebanon, New Jersey, with their six children and numerous gerbils.